THE ART OF FACILITATION

Yamini Hundare

Made with ♥ on the Notion Press Platform
www.notionpress.com

Optimising team meetings and retrospectives by harnessing the power of effective meeting strategies, collaborative activities and templates.

DEDICATION

Dedicated to change. As we all know, change is the only constant, and changing with time is the greatest achievement. Change can be difficult, but it's the most beautiful transition.

Table of Contents

INTRODUCTION **8**

TYPES OF MEETINGS **9**

In-person meetings *10*
Virtual meetings *11*
Hybrid meetings *12*

THE PURPOSE OF THINKING PAGE **14**

EFFECTIVE MEETING STRATEGIES **17**

Timer *17*
Prep work *19*
Instructions *21*
Boundaries *23*
Parking lot *24*
Summarising *25*
Decisions *27*
Breaks *28*
Voting *29*
Tagging *30*
Powerful questions *31*
Spin the wheel *32*
Ambience or Environment *33*
Movements *34*
Rules *36*
Ownership *38*
Grouping *39*
Inclusion *41*

TEAM COLLABORATIVE ACTIVITIES **44**

Check-in Questions *44*
Re-Re Bongo *49*
Think out of the box *53*
My N.A.M.E *58*
Bla. Bla. game *63*
Circle of Positivity *67*
Inner Guru *70*
Just Breathe!!! *73*
Draw <TOPIC> Monster *77*
Find The Person *80*
Yes, But... Yes, And.. *83*
Shiny Star And Stinky Fish *87*
Roll a story *91*
What Do You Need... *96*
Something nice to say... *99*

RETROSPECTIVE TEMPLATES **103**

TYPES OF RETROSPECTIVES 103
Open Retrospectives *103*
Topic specific Retrospectives *104*
Team Retrospectives *105*
AFLI (ASSUMPTIONS | FACTS | LEARNINGS | IMPROVEMENTS) 108
Facilitation *109*
BOOK COVER 111
Facilitation: *112*
HOT AIR BALLOON 115
Facilitation: *115*
PSYCHOLOGICAL SAFETY 118
Facilitation *119*
SPOT LIGHT: TO MAINTAIN FOCUS 122
Facilitation *122*
HIKING RETROSPECTIVE 125
Facilitation *125*

Abstract ladder - Why | What | How	129
Facilitation	*130*
Divest | Invest | Loan	132
Facilitation	*132*
Mindmap	135
Facilitation	*136*
The Sprint Itinerary	138
Facilitation	*139*
Sugar & Salt	142
Facilitation	*143*
Let's Craft With Shapes	146
Facilitation	*147*
Questionnaire	150
Facilitation:	*151*
The Journey	153
Facilitation:	*154*
Roll The Dice And Talk For 1 Min	156
Facilitations	*157*
PAC-MAN	160
Facilitation	*160*
Snakes and Ladder	163
Facilitation	*164*
G.R.O.W	167
Facilitation	*168*
4S	170
Facilitation	*171*
POSTCARD	173
Facilitation	*173*
Start - Improve - Continue	176
Facilitation	*177*

ACKNOWLEDGMENTS

I would like to take this opportunity to express my gratitude to everyone who helped me along the way as I wrote this book. I am deeply grateful to my parents and my extended family for their unwavering love and support, and to my better half, Nikhil, for taking care of our children so I could finish writing this book. Without my amazing teammates and mentors, none of this would have been possible.

It's been more than two years since I started on this journey of documenting and writing about my learning experiences. The initial steps were undeniably the most challenging; it wasn't the act of writing itself that posed difficulties, but rather gathering the courage to share my thoughts with the world. The nagging uncertainty about how my words would be received and the potential judgments from my readers weighed on my mind. If you ask me today, I will say starting as early as possible, delaying won't help, gathering experience and learning from your own mistakes plays the key role in improving. As a reader of this book, I hope you find it interesting and insightful. Please take a moment to reach out and share with me which part or activity in the book resonated with you the most. Your feedback means the world to me, and I am eager to hear your thoughts. Thank you for joining me on this journey, and I look forward to your valuable insights and comments.

I would like to specially thank Canva & Miro. As most of my illustrations are created using Canva and virtual meeting strategies based on Miro or Microsoft Teams.

LinkedIn: https://www.linkedin.com/in/yamini-hundare/
Medium: https://medium.com/@yamini-hundare

Introduction

In the fast-paced and ever-evolving in-person, virtual or hybrid world of business, effective teamwork and collaboration are vital for success. The ability to lead and facilitate productive team meetings and retrospectives is a skill that can set you apart as a dynamic and effective leader. "The Art Of Facilitation" is your guide to achieving just that.

Based on my practical experience in facilitating in-person, virtual or hybrid team meetings and retrospectives, this book explores the strategies and templates that can transform your meetings into dynamic, engaging, and productive experiences. *This results in enhanced team dynamics, improved problem-solving, and ultimately, better outcomes for your projects and initiatives.*

The first section of the book is dedicated to Effective Meeting Strategies. It talks about the art of facilitating meetings in an effective way that helps improve the overall outcome of team meetings and enhances the participant’s engagement.

The second part of the book shifts the focus to Team Collaborative Activities. These activities are not just about fun; they serve as catalysts for improved teamwork and problem-solving. From icebreakers that set the stage for productive discussions to energisers that revitalise the team, this section provides a collection of activities for various situations and team sizes. You'll discover how to transform a group of individuals into a cohesive, high-performing team.

The final section of the book is dedicated to Retrospective Templates, a powerful tool for continuous improvement. Retrospectives are the cornerstone of progress, providing a structured way to reflect on past experiences, identify opportunities for growth, and drive positive change. These templates are crafted based on practical experience. You will gain invaluable knowledge and tools from each section, enabling you to confidently facilitate and inspire your team to success.

Types of meetings

If we want to talk about effective templates and collaborative activities, it is critical to first understand the environment in which they will be implemented.
Post covid meetings and the tools we use during these meetings have evolved. The facilitation strategy must be modified depending on the type of meeting being facilitated.

In-person meetings

In-person meetings involve participants gathering physically at a designated location, such as a conference room, office space, or even an interesting external location. They provide face-to-face interaction, allowing for direct communication, body language observation, immediate engagement, and better nonverbal communication.

Making use of the physical space, including activities that promote movements are great for in-person meetings.

It is critical that participants realise that the planned meeting is an in-person meeting; therefore, include the phrase *"In-Person"* in the meeting invite title and clearly mention the location. Given the opportunity also try to verbally reinstate that the meeting is in-person.

Virtual meetings

Virtual meetings take place entirely online, with participants joining remotely from different locations using video conferencing tools or collaboration platforms. They offer convenience and flexibility, eliminating the need for physical travel. The facilitator can also make use of various digital modes to enhance the virtual experience such as video clips, audio clips, digital tools, online gaming platform and more. using giphy's, emojis, stickers, and other digital elements can make digital activities and interactions more engaging and fun.

Setting expectations for camera on or off is one of the most crucial topics for virtual meetings. Instead of being decided at random, there must be an agreement. In one-on-one meetings, it's preferable to see the other person rather than converse with a blank screen, but there may be situations in which this is not required. It's critical to clarify these standards.

Hybrid meetings

Hybrid meetings combine elements of both virtual and in-person meetings. Some participants join remotely, while others are physically present at a specific location. Hybrid gatherings are the most challenging to facilitate. As the facilitator doesn't want to lose the momentum of an in-person connection, but also needs to include virtual participants. The facilitator is expected to strike a balance between in-person and virtual elements so that no participant feels isolated or disconnected.

In hybrid meetings, it's crucial to avoid the scenario where in-person participants are merely sitting in a room all logged into a virtual meeting, as this can diminish the benefits of in-person interaction. To create a more balanced and engaging hybrid meeting environment it is important to have the right infrastructure such as a centralised TV Unit or a large display unit in the meeting room that allows the in-person and virtual participants to see each other clearly.

A facilitator has a vital role in managing hybrid meetings. Making certain that the actual sticky notes and virtual discussions are collaborated in such a way that both sets of participants can contribute. Participants in person can use sticky notes on a physical board, whilst virtual participants can use a digital platform with chats and virtual sticky notes.

The purpose of Thinking Page

When I am discussing collaborative activities, I have included facilitation strategies for different meeting types. After describing the activity and sharing my experience, I have added a "Thinking Page", a blank canvas to take notes or to create your own version of the activity. During one of my learning workshops, I discovered the power of writing. When you write or teach about something, you process the same information multiple times in various ways, which helps it stick to your mind. It is learning techniques that reinforce understanding and promote deeper learning. So hopefully the Thinking Page will help you go over the knowledge you captured in multiple ways, making it stick more and more. I have also added "Thinking Page" after every retrospective template that is shared in this book. You can note down your experience of facilitating the specific retrospective activity and note down improvements. For example, use of timers could have helped the participants to set boundaries and manage time efficiently.

This book can also be treated as a practice journal, note down your learning and observations on the thinking page gathered from your experience of facilitating the particular activity. This will help in creating a learning journey, Thinking Page is your opportunity to be creative, to note your learning, and to share your experience. Revisiting the Thinking Page can be valuable in contributing to your personal and professional growth.

THINKING PAGE

Add your own effective meeting strategies to help with facilitation.

Effective Meeting Stratergies

Effective Meeting Strategies

Timer

Ensure that the meeting or activity stays on schedule. Timers can be particularly useful for time-sensitive activities or when there are multiple agenda items that need to be addressed within a limited timeframe.

When using timers, it's important to consider the team size and the type of meeting. For larger teams or virtual meetings, it may be necessary to allow more time for discussions and interactions, so you can adjust the timer accordingly. In-person activities often incorporate movements and small talk, which can affect the timing as well.

There are various tools you can use to set timers, depending on the context. If you're facilitating a virtual meeting, many collaboration tools have built-in timer features that you can utilise. Alternatively, you can use your phone or a stopwatch to keep track of the time.

If the timer is not visible to the participants, it's good practice to remind them when it's halfway through the allotted time or when there are only a few minutes remaining. This helps participants stay aware of the time constraints and encourages them to wrap up their current tasks or discussions. As a facilitator, it also allows you to monitor the progress and adjust if needed to keep the meeting on track.

Use of silent timers, writing down the remaining time on a paper and moving around to make sure the participants can read. The font should be big and the writing should be clear for the participants to read from a distance. For example, Last 2 MIN written on a A4 size paper big enough and in bold letters making it clearly visible. Also restrict the message to a couple of words. This practice avoids interrupting discussions.

Overall, incorporating timers into your facilitation process can enhance time management, increase productivity, and ensure that all agenda items are addressed within the allocated time frame. It also improves overall focus.

Prep work

When facilitating meetings, training sessions or workshops that might be In-Person, Virtual or Hybrid events need some preparation or homework done by the participants.

- Clearly communicate the need for pre-meeting preparation or homework in the meeting invite. Don't assume that participants will automatically complete the tasks.
- Even with reminders, some participants may enter the meeting without completing the prep work. Be prepared to handle this situation. We are all guilty of walking into a meeting without going through the agenda so be prepared some participants might miss the details mentioned in the email completely.
- Participants may choose to ignore the email's text content, but occasionally a visual clue makes it easier for them to understand. Make it loud (visually), add an image, a giphy, or use emojis to make it more prominent.
- Have extra copies of documents or materials on hand that you can distribute to participants who

haven't completed the preparation. This ensures that they can still participate in the meeting.

- While you can encourage participants to come prepared, avoid making it a compulsion. People have varying circumstances and constraints that may affect their ability to complete prep work. Encourage participants to be prepared through motivation, inspiration, and gentle reminders. Create a positive environment that fosters cooperation.
- If participants haven't completed prep work, consider setting consequences that don’t feel like punishments but serve as reminders. For instance, reduce break times slightly to accommodate extra time needed to catch up on the pre-meeting materials. Use consequences to highlight the importance of being prepared rather than as punishment. Emphasise that preparedness is part of the expected behaviour in the meeting.

By following these guidelines, you can create a more inclusive and effective meeting environment, ensuring that participants are engaged and able to contribute even if they haven't completed the prep work. This approach promotes collaboration and understanding while recognizing that not everyone may be able to meet the same level of preparation.

Instructions

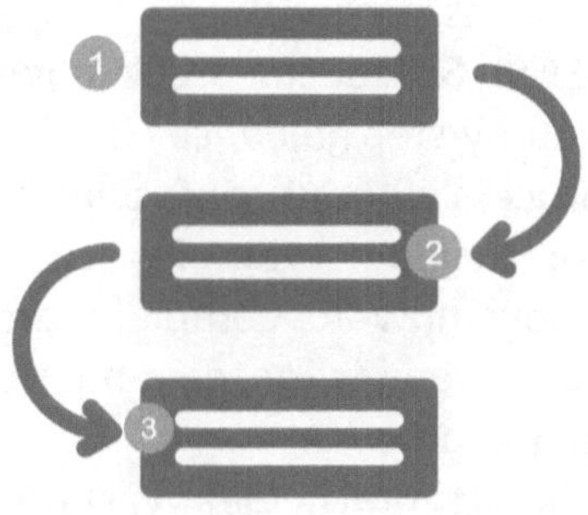

Instructions are often overlooked in team meetings, despite being one of the most important factors in the meeting's success. It is critical to deliver direction not just verbally but also in text or graphic format that is immediately apparent to the team. During retrospectives, the team is given several directions, and remembering all of the metaphors while also brainstorming is tough; therefore, adding instructions that describe what the team is expected to contribute with regard to various metaphors is critical. Otherwise, the team may misinterpret the exercise, and you, as a facilitator, will miss out on vital input.

Here are some best practices for providing instructions effectively:

Written Instructions: Provide written instructions in a format that's easily visible to the team. Physical display on whiteboards, posters or digitally.

Visual Aids: Visual aids can significantly enhance understanding. Consider using diagrams, flowcharts, or visual metaphors that illustrate the instructions. Visual aids make complex concepts easy to understand.

Clear Language: Use simple and clear language when providing instructions. Avoid jargon or technical terms that may confuse team members. Ensure that everyone can understand the instructions.

Step-by-Step Guidance: Break down the instructions into clear, step-by-step guidance. This helps team members follow the process without confusion.

Examples: Include examples to illustrate what is expected. Show how to complete the task or activity. Examples make it easier for team members to understand and replicate the process.

Explicit Expectations: Clearly state what you expect from the team. Define what they need to share, how to share it, and what the desired outcome of the activity is. Be explicit about your expectations.

Questions and Clarifications: Encourage team members to ask questions if they need clarification. Make sure they feel comfortable seeking guidance when necessary.

Feedback Loop: After providing the instructions, ask if there are any questions or concerns. This provides an opportunity for team members to seek clarification and ensures everyone is on the same page.

Consistency: Use a consistent format for providing instructions, so the team becomes familiar with the structure and can anticipate what to expect.

Reinforcement: Repeat important instructions and key points throughout the meeting. Repetition helps reinforce understanding.

Timing: Providing instructions right before the activity is ideal. This ensures that the instructions are fresh in the participants' minds, and they can start the activity with a clear understanding of what's expected.

Feedback Gathering: After the activity or task is

completed, gather feedback from the team regarding the clarity and effectiveness of the instructions. Use this feedback to improve instructions in future meetings.

Boundaries

Boundaries during meetings refer to the guidelines and limits that help ensure that the meeting is conducted effectively and respectfully. Setting boundaries is crucial for successful meetings. It helps ensure that meetings are productive, efficient, and respectful of everyone's time and contributions. Clearly define the purpose of the meeting and create an agenda. Share this agenda with participants in advance so they know what to expect and can prepare accordingly. Stick to the agenda during the meeting to avoid going off track. They help prevent time-wasting, keep discussions on track, and ensure that meetings achieve their intended goals. Additionally, respecting boundaries contributes to a positive and professional meeting environment. Encourage the participants to highlight when the defined boundaries are not respected. This can only be achieved in a safe environment.

Parking lot

Before beginning a meeting, introduce the parking lot and dedicate a specific space. It can be a small square marked on your whiteboard or a frame drawn on your virtual board. It helps in creating an effective way to manage discussions and ensure that valuable topics or ideas are not disregarded or forgotten.

By acknowledging ideas or topics that are outside the current scope of the discussion and "parking" them in a designated space, you create a sense of inclusion and respect for the participants. This approach allows everyone to feel heard and valued, even if their ideas are not immediately relevant to the ongoing conversation.

Furthermore, the parking lot provides a mechanism for addressing those parked topics or ideas at a later time. At the end of the meeting or discussion, you can review the items in the parking lot and determine what actions should be taken. This may involve scheduling dedicated follow-up discussions, assigning specific individuals to explore those ideas further, or incorporating them into future agendas.

By utilising a parking lot, you foster an environment where people feel encouraged to express their opinions and ideas without fear of immediate dismissal. This can help build trust within the group and lead to more productive and inclusive discussions in the long run.

Summarising

Summarising is a valuable skill that can greatly improve one-on-one communication, meetings, presentations, or even written documents. It involves capturing the main points, key ideas, and essential details of a discussion or text in a concise and coherent manner. It focuses on filtering out important details and avoiding repetition. It assists in providing a clear and concise snapshot of the discussion. It helps retain information that can be carried forward. Some meetings are difficult to wrap up in one go and may extend into multiple meetings; summarising at the end of such meetings is critical to retain the context and helps in continuation. The communication thread can be picked up from the point where it was left.

In virtual meetings, it is often found that participants add multiple sticky notes, at the end of the meeting it is important to identify which topics are covered and which are pending. This can either be done by changing the colour of the sticky notes. The topics that are already discussed change the colour of those sticky notes and add a summary of the discussion. This will help to continue the discussion from where it left off. Before warping up the meeting allows participants to add some context to the sticky notes that are not discussed. So, during the next meeting it becomes easy to recollect. One liners or a couple of words might not help recollect the context. Adding author name or tag on sticky notes is helpful to recollect who wrote the sticky note.

Similarly, during in-person meetings, make sure to segregate topics that have already been discussed from those that still need to be discussed. It helps enhance the overall experience for the participants. As a facilitator, you feel more confident to continue the discussion across multiple meetings.

Decisions

Asking clarifying questions and reaching conclusions is a powerful skill that can transform the way teams interact, make decisions, and solve problems. It is about asking the right questions and navigating the discussion towards a conclusion. Making conscious, well informed decisions is important for team alignment. It helps prevent topics from falling through the cracks and keeps the conversation on track. This practice promotes effective communication and decision-making. During team meetings it is often observed that topics or questions get raised and somewhere they also get dropped off the radar, this can be quite vague and random. When a topic or question gets raised it is important to ask if this is important to be discussed? Should this be added to a parking lot with a dedicated assigned owner or schedule a follow up discussion? It is also okay to admit that it is not important and can be dropped off the radar. But this has to be a conscious decision not a default decision in case if no one has the answer. It is important to identify what should be the next step in such a scenario.

Breaks

The power of breaks should not be underestimated. By incorporating regular intervals for participants to disconnect, take a short break, attend to personal needs, and hydrate, you can prevent these minor distractions from hindering engagement. There are scientific studies that support the fact that attention span starts to decrease after 20 minutes. The number can vary between the studies, but the facts remain the same. Breaks help reset the participant's attention span. Breaks are also good if the tension is rising or if there is a heated argument. It gives time for the participants to calm down. It is a good practice to announce in the beginning that there would be breaks during the meeting. Setting expectations and avoiding unnecessary surprises helps improve the experience for the participants.

Voting

Voting can be an effective tool for improving focus, prioritising topics, and understanding the needs of a group during brainstorming sessions. It fosters collaboration, inclusivity, and efficient use of time, ultimately leading to better decision-making. It ensures that every individual has an equal opportunity to contribute to the decision-making process. It creates a visual representation, or "heat map", of the participant's preferences. During workshops, training, team meetings, or retrospectives. Voting can be used to improve focus and time-management, allowing every participant to contribute. It ensures that everyone's input is considered and helps to avoid the dominance of a few loud individuals. When there are more topics to be discussed and it is not possible to address all of them within the timebox. Ask the participants to vote for the most important topics and focus on it rather than trying to tackle everything and not getting anything done. Participants can make use of digital tools for voting or can use voting dots to do the same.

Tagging

Tagging is a simple yet valuable technique that can be used in group discussions. This approach helps in a smooth, organised and inclusive conversation. As the facilitator, you select the first person to begin the discussion. This can be done randomly. The initial speaker shares their input or responds to a question. After they finish, they "tag" the next person to speak. This can be done by calling their name or simply indicating that it's their turn. The tagged person then provides their input, and after they finish, they tag the next person to speak. This process continues until everyone in the group has had the opportunity to share their input or until the discussion reaches its conclusion.

It ensures that the discussion flows in an organised manner, with each person taking their turn. No overlapping, it reduces the chances of multiple people speaking at once, which can cause confusion and disrupt the discussion. Everyone in the group gets a chance to participate, preventing dominant voices from hijacking the conversation. It can help maintain a reasonable pace and avoid long pauses. It makes it clear who should speak next, eliminating the need for participants to decide who goes first.

Powerful questions

Powerful questions can prove to be very effective in leading the discussion in the right direction. It can help improve the overall facilitation experience for the participants. The questions depend on the context and dynamics of the team; there is no defined set of powerful questions. These questions support the team in brainstorming, unblocking, being creative, motivating, and encouraging. Powerful questions can foster a positive and collaborative atmosphere, encourage active engagement from all participants, and unlock insights that might not surface through ordinary discussions. Asking these open-ended and thought-provoking questions can help in exploring different perspectives, challenging assumptions, and uncovering underlying issues or opportunities for improvement. It simulates meaningful dialog during a discussion.

For example,

- Can you explain or elaborate?
- Can you provide an example?
- What is the biggest challenge that we might encounter?
- What is the success criteria?
- Can we measure success?
- How can we accelerate the process/project?
- What would the completed project look like?
- What should be the outcome of this task/project/discussion?

Spin the wheel

Using a random selection method like "Spin the Wheel" can be a fun and effective way to choose participants or make selections during various activities, meetings, or events. This approach minimises potential biases and adds an element of gamification to the process. It is a very simple but effective selection process. It can be especially useful for activities where random selection is essential, such as choosing a team leader, someone who can kick-start a discussion, or a presenter. It helps create a positive and unbiased atmosphere in meetings and events. There are a number of online tools that can be used. I have been successfully using picker-wheel to pick the sprint review presenter for one of my teams. Using this method everyone on the team gets an opportunity, we also skip the last presenter from the list to make sure the same person is not picked up back-to-back.

Ambience or Environment

The ambiance and environment play a significant role in influencing behaviour and productivity. Companies invest in creative and thoughtfully designed spaces because they recognise the impact that the physical environment has on employees and their work. It helps boost creativity, overall productivity, and inspirational thinking. This is applicable for in-person or hybrid meetings; virtual meetings might have to settle with creative backgrounds.

A thoughtfully designed meeting environment can enhance the overall meeting experience in several ways. It can be refreshing and uplifting to have a meeting in a well-designed space.

Well-lit, comfortable, and colourful meeting room can help participants have more collaborative and engaging interactions. Having natural elements like fresh air, plants, and sunlight can help boost the participant's mood.

Movements

Using the space and incorporating movements can significantly enhance engagement and active listening during meetings or presentations. Incorporating movements and effective use of the space can transform a meeting or event into a more engaging and participatory experience. It not only holds the participants attention but also fosters active listening, interaction, and a deeper connection between the participants. Indeed, sitting in one place for an extended period can lead to fatigue and reduced engagement during discussions or meetings. Introducing movement and activities that boost creativity can strengthen participant engagement and enhance the quality of discussions. For example, during an in-person meeting if you ask the participant to rate their satisfaction on a scale of 1 to 5 by moving on a physical line representing the scale rather than simply saying it verbally makes it more impactful and engaging. Here you are combining virtual representation with verbal communication.

Rules

Sharing a list of minimal rules to maintain the decorum of the meeting or to set expectations. By sharing and adhering to minimal rules, teams can create a respectful and productive meeting environment that contributes to team morale and overall effectiveness. These rules can differ as per the team and the activity.

Few examples:

- **Be On Time:** Start and end meetings promptly to respect everyone's time. Arrive on time and encourage others to do the same.
- **Prepare Ahead:** Come to the meeting prepared with any necessary materials, reports, or updates.
- **Stay Engaged:** Pay attention and actively participate. Avoid multitasking or distractions, such as checking emails or social media.
- **Respect Others' Speaking Time:** Allow each person to speak without interruption. Raise your hand or use a designated system if there are multiple speakers.
- **Listen Actively:** Show respect by actively listening

to what others are saying. Avoid side conversations.

- **Stay on Topic:** Stick to the meeting agenda and avoid going off on unrelated tangents.
- **One Conversation at a Time:** Avoid speaking over others. Wait for your turn to contribute.
- **Use Constructive Language:** Be mindful of your tone and choice of words. Offer constructive feedback and avoid negativity.
- **Disagree Respectfully:** It's okay to have differing opinions but express them respectfully. Avoid personal attacks.
- **Limit Use of Jargon:** Ensure that everyone can understand the discussion by minimising the use of industry-specific jargon or acronyms or short forms.
- **Raise Concerns Respectfully:** If you have concerns or disagreements, raise them in a polite and constructive manner.
- **Follow Up on Action Items:** If you commit to action items during the meeting, follow through on them by the agreed-upon deadlines.
- **No Blame, Focus on Solutions:** Instead of blaming, focus on finding solutions to challenges or issues.
- **Respect Meeting Time:** Stick to the scheduled meeting duration. If more time is needed, schedule a follow-up meeting.
- **Use Technology Mindfully**: If using virtual meeting tools, mute your microphone when not speaking and avoid excessive background noise.
- **Be Inclusive:** Encourage everyone to participate, especially quieter team members. Ensure that all voices are heard.
- **Stay Positive:** Maintain a positive and collaborative

attitude, even when discussing difficult topics.

- **Feedback is Welcome:** Encourage open feedback about the meeting format and effectiveness to continuously improve.
- **This is a safe space:** Please speak openly and honestly.
- **No judgement:** We may have different opinions, and that's ok.
- **Be kind:** We know things aren't perfect, but we're here to make things better.

Ownership

When we talk about meetings, events or action items ownership comes uninvited. There is a very thin line between the role and responsibilities Vs Ownership. When ownership walks along responsibility that's when the magic happens. When an individual takes ownership they not only acknowledge their responsibility but also demonstrate a sense of commitment and personal investment in the task's success. During meetings, discussions or retrospectives when action items are derived it is recommended to assign these action items to owners. Owners are not expected to do the entire work, but they are held responsible for the outcome of the action item. signoffs and setting clear expectations can play a significant role in reinforcing ownership and accountability within a team.

Grouping

Participants in team building exercises, meetings, training sessions, or workshops must be divided into smaller groups for discussions or activities. To avoid the difficult discussion about whether I should join or whether we should do it together. The more outgoing audience members typically form groups, which makes them a dominant group. Use grouping techniques to ensure that participants are evenly distributed and have equal opportunities. This tedious task can be made more enjoyable and straightforward by using simple grouping approaches. A few grouping techniques are listed below.

- Counting in base 10, For instance, you must divide the participants into smaller groups. Ask the participants to begin counting from 1 to 3, ask them to keep going until each person has received one number. Now instruct the participants to divide into groups according to numbers. All 1s combined, all 2s combined, and the same is true for the number 3 participants. The range of counting numbers will change based on how many audiences and groups you wish to include. You can also make use of alphabets in a similar manner.
- Using colourful objects and small objects to form groups is not only a creative way to organise participants but also adds a fun and memorable element to your event. Gather a variety of small objects in different colours or types. You can use bouncy balls in various colours, pom-poms in different shades, or mini figures of the same type (e.g., animals or characters). As participants arrive, instruct each person to select one object from the bowl. Once everyone has chosen an object, ask participants to form groups based on the colour or type of the object they picked. For example, all those with red objects form one group, and those with blue objects create another group. To make the experience even more engaging and memorable, consider gifting these small objects to participants as event souvenirs.

Inclusion

While designing workshops, training sessions, planning meetings or facilitating, make sure your base is always the principle of inclusivity. Equal opportunity makes an individual feel valued and motivates them to contribute during team events. Promote active listening, use inclusive language, embrace diversity of thoughts, respect regional and cultural variations, use silent brainstorming techniques to allow introverted team members to contribute their ideas uninterrupted, and promote equal speaking time. Inclusion is a by-product of using efficient meeting strategies. Be considerate while selecting a location, time or technology for meetings.

Inclusion in meetings is an ongoing effort that requires commitment from leadership and active participation from all team members. When everyone feels valued and heard, it can lead to more innovative solutions, stronger team relationships, and better overall outcomes.

Thinking Page

Add your own effective meeting strategies to help with facilitation.

Team collaborative activities

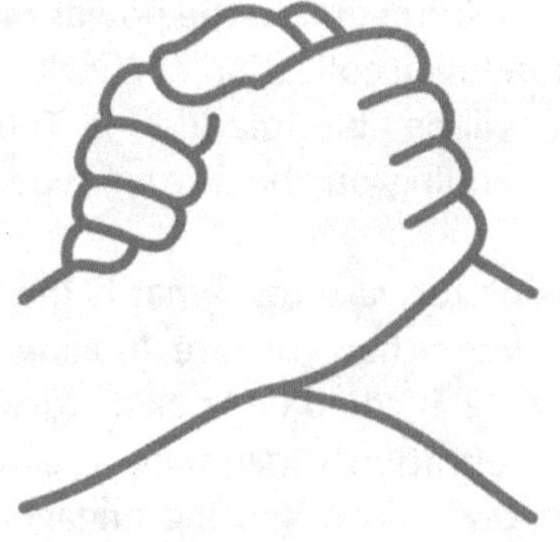

Team Collaborative Activities

Check-in Questions

"Check-in Question" is a simple and effective activity which can work with just two people or even a bigger audience. It plays a crucial role in building connections and fostering effective communication. It can serve as an excellent icebreaker and a way to introduce a topic for further small talk. Small talk helps weave the communication threads and these threads are the basis of the communication fabric. Never underestimate the power of small talk.

I have listed below a collection of check-in questions, and I am sure you will be able to add to it. These questions will also vary depending on the size or type of audience you have.

- Looking forward to... what is the next big, exciting life event that you are looking forward to? For example, it could be Looking forward to some sort of celebration, upcoming vacation plan, buying your own place, getting engaged, your next SPA appointment or even something as simple as relaxing over the weekend.
- When was the last time you remember you laughed your lungs out, rolled on the floor and laughed till your stomach hurt?
- Fun Facts... Share a fun fact about yourself, the current sprint or project. This question is a super hit and through these fun facts you discover something new and interesting about a person or even a sprint or a project.
- What is your easy-peasy go to food? Something that is quick, easy and your default choice when

you run out of options.

- What is your comfort food?
- What is your hidden talent or skill?
- Any new hobbies or interests you have picked up recently?
- What is a recent accomplishment you are proud of?
- What is your favourite fitness activity?
- Share a happy memory?
- Do you play any sport and what is that?
- What is the best advice you have ever received?
- What is the goal that you want to achieve, and you are struggling with?

When dealing with a large group of participants, using simple questions with limited options like "Yes/No" or "Agree/Disagree" questions can be more practical. Here are some additional check-in questions, including those with binary responses, that work well in larger group settings. These questions are designed to be easy to answer with limited options and can quickly engage a larger group of participants. They can help initiate group discussions or icebreakers while respecting time constraints. Depending on the audience and context, you can choose questions that are most relevant and interesting for the group.

- Are you a morning or night person?
- Do you prefer tea or coffee?
- Did you have your breakfast today?
- Are you a dog or cat person?
- Do you enjoy cooking?
- Do you enjoy gardening?
- Are you a fan of international cuisines?
- Are you an early planner or last min decision maker?

- Are you an introvert or extrovert?
- Do you believe in spending or investing?

In-Person: This activity works well in both in-person and virtual setup. During in-person meetings try to combine it with some movements which add to the dynamics of the activity and make it more engaging. For example: Pop-Corn Pop-Up, the participants can quickly stand up representing a Popcorn that Pops-Up and share his/her response. If done in a quick fashion it seems like Popping Popcorns.

Virtual: Check-in questions can also be used as fillers, since we adapted the hybrid way of working or moved towards more virtual meeting people usually can be a couple of mins late or in case of you are waiting for someone to join and cannot proceed, using check-in question can be a great way to engage the audience and use this time to initiate some small talk.

You can design multiple forms of this activity to make it more interesting.

- **Turn a card:** Add one inquiry question per card. Create multiple cards with different questions. Place them upside down in a stack. Ask your team to sit in a circle. Let them draw a card and answer the inquiry questions. For virtual meetings create a grid of upside-down cards using a digital tool. Now ask the participants to turn the cards and answer the inquiry question.

- **The bowl of inquiry:** Write down inquiry questions on multiple pieces of papers or print multiple inquiry questions and cut them out. Now fold these pieces of paper and add it to a bowl. Let the participants pick a folder piece of paper and answer the inquiry question. For a virtual meeting you can cover the questions and let the participants uncover and answer them, you can add some drama to it with virtual tools.

THINKING PAGE

Add your personal touch of creativity to the activity to craft your unique version.

Re-Re Bongo

Relate – **Re**pel (I added 'Bongo' just for fun so that the name sticks to your mind.)

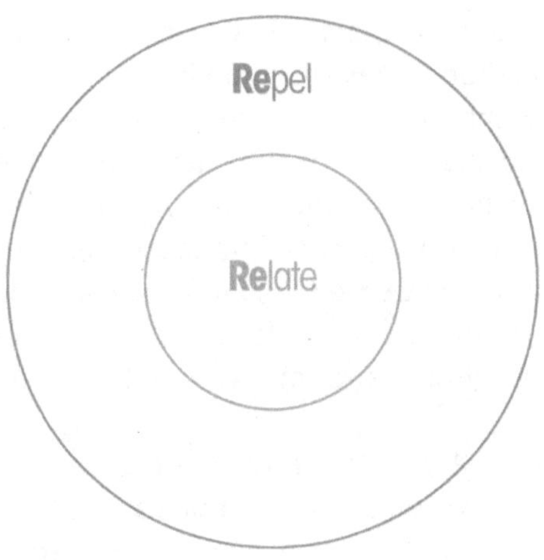

This activity, which is a heat map or a data visualisation tool, can be a fun and engaging way to gather insights and encourage interaction among participants. By positioning a question or topic at the centre and asking participants to move towards or away from the centre based on their level of agreement or preference, you create a visual

representation of their responses.
Using this activity for voting or polls can help you quickly gauge the collective opinion or preference of the group. It can also serve as an icebreaker, allowing participants to connect over shared interests or opinions.
Re-Re Bongo as a quick energizer: Make a list of 10 questions. If the participant related to the question, they would move toward the centre; if they do not relate to it, they will move away from the centre. Depending on how much the participants relate to or repel it, they should position themselves based on it.
For example: If you want to know if your teammates are coffee lovers, just ask the question, “I love my coffee.” Based on how much they love it, they move either towards the centre or, if a participant doesn’t like coffee at all, they move to the extreme end, far away from the centre.
This activity is great for both in-person and virtual meetings. It promotes movement if it’s in person.

In-Person: If you can draw a circle or stick a tape on the floor, that is great; if not, just place an object in the middle, or as a facilitator, just stand in the centre of the room representing the Relate circle and ask the participants to either move closer towards the centre or away from it depending on how much they relate to or repel the topic/question. In case doing it in circles is not feasible you can also do it with a vertical or a horizontal line, by sticking sticky notes on the floor in a line with numbers say 1 to 5, where 1 indicates you agree and 5 indicates you disagree and all the other values in between. You can use smiley faces on the sticky notes in a similar manner instead of numbers. Explore and think about different ways you can facilitate and use this activity during your meetings.

Virtual: I have used MIRO as a collaboration tool for virtual meetings. Drawing the Re-Re Bongo circle is super easy to do using MIRO. Let the participants choose an icon, avatar, or emoji, and let them move it towards the related or repel circles.

Board created in MIRO

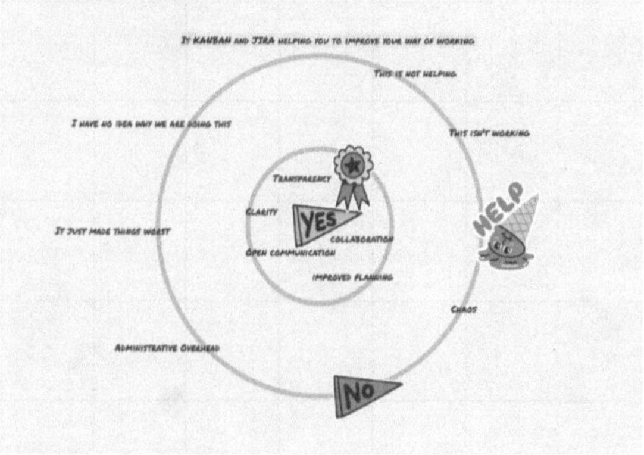

While facilitating the virtual psychological retrospective, I twigged the activity further. I asked the participants to place their avatars based on the general feeling of safety they have when working within the team. But I also asked the participants if they have experienced any specific incidents, situations, or behaviours that threatened their safety or helped them feel safer. In this case, the position of the avatar shows how the participant feels 80% of the time, but those 20% of incidents that have a lasting positive or negative impact are important to capture. So, the extra sticky note highlights those 20% impacting experiences. You can twig the Re-Re Bongo activity in many possible ways.

Thinking Page

Add your personal touch of creativity to the activity to craft your unique version.

Think out of the box

Just as the name suggests, this activity is a creative exercise that encourages participants to think outside the box and embrace their individual perspectives and creativity. It reminds us that everyone has their own unique way of doing things.

To conduct the activity, follow these steps:

- Prepare the half-done picture: Create a drawing of an octopus and complete only half of it, leaving the other half unfinished.
- Share the half-done picture: Display the half-done picture to the participants, ensuring everyone can see it clearly. Explain that the objective is to guess what the original drawing is based on the visible half.

- Guessing the original drawing: Give participants a few minutes to individually guess what they think the complete drawing could be. Do not discuss it or share it.

- Sharing and creating a new drawing: After the guessing phase, ask each participant to create a completely new drawing using the half-done picture as a starting point. Emphasise that the new drawing should be different from what they initially guessed the original drawing to be.
- Sharing and reflection: Once everyone has completed their new drawings, show the original complete picture. Allow participants to share and explain their creations. This can be done individually or in small groups. Encourage open discussions about the different interpretations and approaches taken by participants. What they thought the original drawing was and what they drew.

This activity promotes creativity, thinking outside the box, and embracing diverse perspectives within a team. It also encourages participants to challenge their assumptions and explore alternative possibilities. By focusing on creating a new drawing rather than guessing the original one, participants are encouraged to tap into their individuality and contribute to the collective creativity of the group.
It also highlights that every individual has his or her own way of thinking and creating. The other side of this activity focuses on assumptions; a half-done drawing or lack of information can lead to assumptions based on which the participants can create their own version of the picture.

In-Person: Make sure you keep multiple copies of the half-done picture ready to be shared with the team. In case you cannot get access to a printer, you can simply draw the half-done drawing on a white board and ask the participants to make the exact drawing on their paper and later complete it.

Virtual: When facilitating the activity virtually, breakout rooms or private mode in MIRO can be super helpful to avoid the participants being influenced by each other's ideas. Participants can also use pen and paper to copy the half-done picture and draw the complete picture, which can be shared via the camera.

Thinking Page

Add your personal touch of creativity to the activity to craft your unique version.

My N.A.M.E

The activity is an excellent ice breaker that allows participants to share interesting facts about themselves while also getting to know each other's names. It's a simple and engaging exercise that can be conducted with no prior preparation and is suitable for both in-person and virtual settings.

To facilitate the activity, follow these steps:

- Explain the instructions: Introduce the activity to the participants. Instruct them to share their first name and an interesting fact about themselves corresponding to each letter of their name. Emphasise that the facts should be unknown to the rest of the group, creating an element of surprise.
- Model the activity: Start by sharing your own name and interesting facts corresponding to each letter of your name. This will provide an example for the participants and set the tone for the activity.
- Encourage participation: Invite each participant, one by one, to share their name and the interesting facts about themselves. Create a supportive and inclusive environment that encourages active listening and engagement from the rest of the group.
- Facilitate discussion: After each participant shares their facts, encourage the group to ask questions or make comments, fostering a sense of connection and sparking potential small talk topics for future interactions.
- Reflect and wrap up: Once all participants have shared, take a moment to reflect on the activity as a group. Highlight the diversity of interests and experiences within the team and discuss any commonalities or points of connection that emerged.
- By engaging in this activity, team members will not only learn each other's names but also discover interesting aspects of each other's lives. It helps to foster a sense of familiarity,

encourages conversations beyond work-related topics, and promotes a positive team dynamic.

For example:
Hi, I'm Yamini.
Y "Yak" is a hairy animal, which I rode just once in my life during a trek in the northern part of India. and I do not wish to ride any animals anymore.
A I use the word "Actually" quite often during a conversation. I have tried being mindful about it. But do let me know if you find me doing that.
M is for "Mangoes", Anyone who knows me can tell how much I love Indian mangoes. I used to make a trip to the coastal area of Maharashtra, India - Kokan just to get my favourite mangoes. For 2 to 3 months, my diet included mangoes in some form or the other during the day.
I is for ice cream. I love eating ice cream. Coming from a warm country, that is like a mandate. But my ice cream intake has decreased drastically since I moved to the Netherlands.
N is for Nashik. The city where I was born and brought up.
I is for "INK PENS"; it's been more than a decade since I haven't used ink pens, but I will always have a love for them. I used to love writing with ink pens that were replaced by gel pens, but still, ink pens have a special place in my life.

In-person: Having participants sit in a circle and taking turns to stand and share their name facts maintains a sense of unity and connection within the group. It allows for better visibility and engagement among participants, fostering a positive and interactive environment. To save time, prepare the necessary materials ahead of time by writing the names of the participants vertically on a sheet of paper and handing it over to the appropriate participant. Alternatively, simply give blank sheets and allow participants to create their own.

Virtual: Utilising collaboration tools like MIRO can be a great way to adapt the activity. Creating frames for each participant and using emojis, stickers, and giphys add a fun and creative element to the ice breaker. Activating private mode during the activity allows participants to work on their frames individually, ensuring a surprise factor when they are shared with the group. The frames can serve as a visual representation of each participant's interesting facts, creating a virtual gallery that can be revisited and enjoyed by the team. Creating a separate project or board dedicated to team building activities in MIRO allows for easy organisation and access to these ice breaker frames and other team building exercises.

By incorporating these variations, you enhance the engagement and enjoyment of the ice breaker activity in both in-person and virtual settings, fostering team connectivity and creating a memorable experience for participants.

THINKING PAGE

Add your personal touch of creativity to the activity to craft your unique version.

Bla. Bla. game

The Bla. Bla. game is a fun and interactive way to remind your team about the importance of avoiding excessive abbreviations or short forms without providing context or explanation. It highlights the potential confusion and lack of understanding that can arise when using such abbreviations without considering the audience.

To play the game, follow these steps:

- Introduce the purpose: Explain to the team that the game aims to emphasise the significance of sharing the meaning of abbreviations or short forms when communicating with others.
- Explain the rules: Instruct everyone to write a meaningful sentence by replacing a word within that sentence with the pharse "Bla. Bla.".
- Provide the replacement word: As the facilitator, you should have a specific replacement word in mind for "Bla. Bla." that will be used to replace it in all the sentences. That the participants have written
- Replace "Bla. Bla." in the sentences: Take each individual's sentence and replace "Bla. Bla." with the predetermined replacement word. Make sure the replacement is consistent across all the sentences.
- Read the sentences aloud: As a group, take turns reading the modified sentences out loud. Encourage participants to pay attention to whether the sentences still make sense and if they can understand the intended meaning.
- Reflect and discuss: After reading the sentences, initiate a discussion about the impact of using abbreviations or short forms without providing clear explanations. Encourage participants to share their observations and insights. Emphasise the importance of clarity and avoiding assumptions when communicating with others.

- By engaging in this game, your team can develop a greater awareness of the potential challenges and misunderstandings that can arise from using abbreviations or short forms without context. It serves as a reminder to be mindful and considerate when using such language in order to ensure effective communication with diverse audiences.

In-person: Ask the participants to write one meaningful sentence on a sticky note. While writing this sentence replace one word with the phrase Bla. Bla.
Stick all these stickies and then reveal the replacement word for phrase Bla. Bla. that the facilitator has already picked. Now let every individual read out the sentence they have written replacing the Bla. Bla. phrase with the word. Let the team enjoy some laughter and small talks.

Virtual: Using virtual sticky notes on MIRO, follow the same steps and let the participants discuss the challenges the audience might face when abbreviations and short forms are used. Let them share their learning and experiences.

THINKING PAGE

Add your personal touch of creativity to the activity to craft your unique version.

Circle of Positivity

It is a simple little game but helps to boost the team's morale. The team begins on a positive note.

To play the game, follow these steps:

- Ask a positive question For example:- Why do you love working for this team? or What did you enjoy the most during this sprint?
- Every team member needs to provide unique feedback, no one can repeat what the other person has already said. The feedback needs to be small and crip no storytelling.

In-person: Make the team sit in a circle. Take any prop, a pen, a small toy, literally anything which is small enough that can fit in a hand and can be easily passed on.
The person who holds the prop shares positive feedback and passes the prop to the next person. Continue till every individual within the circle is done providing the feedback. This is like the classic game of passing the passing parcel with a twist.

Virtual: Using tagging mechanism, as a facilitator you pick the first person who begins. Now this person shares her/his feedback and tags the next person. This continues till everyone on the team has got the opportunity to share their feedback. If required use a 15 sec or 20 sec timer to make sure it's short and sweet.

THINKING PAGE

Add your personal touch of creativity to the activity to craft your unique version.

Inner Guru

The activity is a fantastic way to start a conversation on a positive and inspiring note.

The essence of the activity is to tap into each individual's inner wisdom the Inner Guru. Ask participants to share positive thoughts or proverbs that inspire them. Some of which can be truly remarkable and uplifting. It helps to start a conversation by listening to something positive which impacts the overall wellbeing of the participants fostering inspiration.

In-person: Using a whiteboard or a full-size white page to draw a sketch of the meditating guru and then asking participants to write down positive thoughts or proverbs on sticky notes is an excellent approach for an in-person Inner Guru facilitation. This visual and interactive method adds a creative and engaging element to the activity.

Virtual: Using a digital tool to draw a sketch of the meditating guru or using an image of a meditating guru and then asking participants to write down positive thoughts or proverbs on sticky notes is an excellent approach for a virtual Inner Guru facilitation. The approach for facilitating this activity is not impacted much even if it's facilitated in-person or virtually.

THINKING PAGE

Add your personal touch of creativity to the activity to craft your unique version.

Just Breathe!!!

The activity is a wonderful way to promote focus, active listening, and mindfulness at the beginning of a meeting. It creates a mental transition for participants, helping them leave behind distractions and prepare to engage fully in the upcoming discussion.

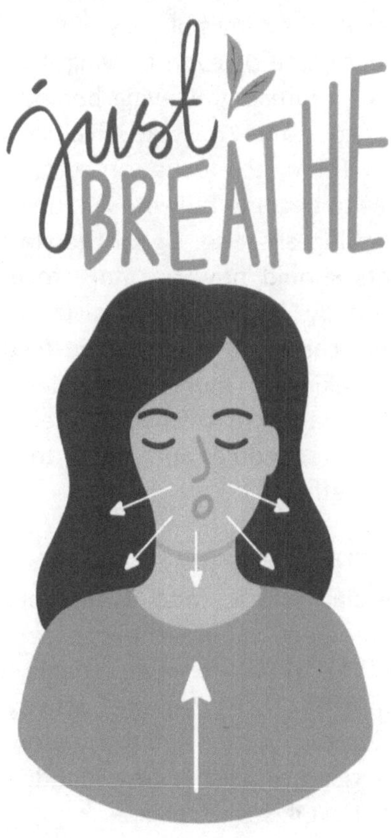

Here's how you can implement this activity. As the facilitator, explain the purpose of the activity. Let participants know that you're going to start the meeting with a mindfulness exercise to help them let go of distractions. Ask participants to imagine they are holding an invisible vessel, a container where they can place their worries and distractions, encouraging them to mentally put these distractions into the vessel. As the facilitator, act as if you are taking their invisible vessel from them and placing it somewhere safe or even burying it in the ground. This symbolic act represents leaving behind their distractions. Instruct participants to take five slow, deep breaths. Encourage them to focus on each breath, allowing themselves to become fully present and centred. After the deep breathing exercise, signal the start of the meeting. Participants should now be more focused and present, having mentally "let go" of their distractions.
This activity can set a positive and focused tone for the meeting, making it more productive and encouraging active participation. It's especially helpful for teams that have a busy schedule and need to transition quickly between meetings.

In-person: The physical and symbolic act of carrying a vessel, placing worries and distractions in it, and then taking a moment to breathe can serve as a powerful reminder and ritual for participants during in-person facilitation of the "Just Breathe" activity. After the act of setting aside the worries and distraction is completed, the participants can practise a few rounds of breathe-in and breathe-out exercises to relax.

Virtually: Facilitating the "Just Breathe" activity in a virtual setting requires some modifications. You can use a digital board with an image of a vessel and ask the participants to write their worries or distractions on a sticky note. Share it with the group and place it on the vessel. At the end you can also make use of an audio clip to help the participants relax and breathe.

Add your personal touch of creativity to the activity to craft your unique version.

Draw <TOPIC> Monster

This activity is engaging and creative that can help teams connect, share their thoughts, and have a bit of fun during a meeting. In the title you can replace <TOPIC> with Sprint, A specific project name, Process, KPI or anything topic the team wants to discuss.

For example:
Draw ***The Sprint*** Monster: The team members are asked to draw an abstract monster based on their imagination that depicts the current sprint. It helps encourage team members to express their thoughts and creativity through drawing and share their perspectives on the sprint in a fun and light-hearted way. The beauty of using a monster theme for this activity is that the emphasis is not on artistic talent but on creativity and expression. This encourages team members to participate without the fear of judgement about their drawing abilities. It's a fun and inclusive way to engage the team in a creative exercise and promote open communication. Plus, the imaginative and often whimsical interpretations of the "Sprint" can lead to interesting and insightful discussions, making it a valuable team building and idea-sharing activity.
After the participants have finished drawing the monsters, they are asked to name them and explain why they appear the way they do.
This activity can also be used as a Retrospective activity.

In-person: If this activity is facilitated in-person, all we need is sheets of white papers, canvas boards, colour pens and some amazing creative minds to bring the monster to life.

Thinking Page

Add your personal touch of creativity to the activity to craft your unique version.

Find The Person

"Find The Person" is a fun and engaging team-building activity that can help discover how well you know your team members. It's a game that can be used in various team settings, such as ice-breaking sessions, team-building workshops, retrospective or as an energiser during meetings.

Find the person

Find the person who matches the description.
The first one who have 5, wins!

Has a pet	Has traveled to more than 5 countries	Is left-handed	Is a vegetarian	Can speak more than one language
Has never been done skying	Has a tattoo	Has a birthday in the same month as you	Has run a marathon	Is a fullstack developer
Is wearing a watch	Has children(s)		Has a fear of heights	Has a famous relative
Is a morning person	Has climbed/hiked a mountain	Plays a musical instrument	Has met a celebrity	Has a unique hobby
Has a graduate degree	Can do a cartwheel	Can juggle	Is a volunteer	Has a birthmark

The participant's task is to find team members who match the descriptions or have experienced what's mentioned in the squares. Participants cannot add their own name. The goal can be to complete a row, a column, just first 5 or 6 squares, or diagonal by finding people who match the descriptions. If possible, giving a little prize to the winner can also be an option.
After the winner is announced, read out each question and ask the team member to raise their hands if they fulfil the criteria. It is fun to find out things we never knew about our fellow team members.

In-person: If this activity is facilitated in-person, printed sheets of the game can be handy to distribute to the participants.

Virtually: For virtual setup keep the one digital copy per participant ready, Try using private mode in MIRO to avoid participants being influenced by each other.

THINKING PAGE

Add your personal touch of creativity to the activity to craft your unique version.

Yes, But... Yes, And..

"Yes, but..." and "Yes, and..." are two contrasting communication techniques that can be used as a fun team activity to highlight the impact of negation and positivity in discussions and problem-solving. This activity can be particularly useful in team building, communication training, or conflict resolution workshops.

Follow the steps to facilitate this activity.

- Explain the purpose of the activity: to understand how negation ("Yes, but...") and positivity ("Yes, and...") affect team interactions and problem-solving.
- Divide the group into pairs or small teams.

Scenario Selection:

Provide each pair or team with a scenario or situation to discuss. This scenario can be a fictional problem, a common workplace challenge, or any topic of interest.

Part 1: "Yes, but...":

Instruct the teams to use the "Yes, but..." approach for this part. Each team should discuss the given scenario by responding to each other's ideas with "Yes, but..." followed by a counterargument or negation. For example, if the scenario is about improving team communication, one person might say, "Yes, but it's difficult because we have remote team members," and the other person might respond with, "Yes, but we can't control their work schedules."

Part 2: "Yes, and...":

Now, ask the teams to switch to the "Yes, and..." approach. In this round, they should discuss the scenario by responding to each other's ideas with "Yes, and..." followed by a positive addition or suggestion. Using the same scenario, one person might say, "Yes, and we can use video calls to connect with remote team members," and the other person might respond with, "Yes, and we can create a shared calendar to manage work schedules collaboratively."

After both rounds, gather the teams back together for a debrief.

Discuss the differences in communication and problem-solving between "Yes, but..." and "Yes, and...". Explore how the "Yes, and..." approach fosters more positive, collaborative, and creative discussions, while "Yes, but..." tends to introduce negativity and resistance.

Encourage the team to reflect on the impact of language and communication on their interactions. Discuss how the "Yes, and..." approach can be used to improve teamwork, brainstorming, and solution-finding.

This activity is a light-hearted way to illustrate the importance of positive and constructive communication within a team. It helps participants experience the impact of negation and the power of positivity in discussions and collaborative problem-solving.

In-person: If this activity is facilitated in-person, split the large group in pairs or small teams. Give a common scenario and ask the team to build on it, using the Yes, But .... approach. After a couple of min instruct the pair or the group to build on the previous scenario using the Yes, And.. approach. There will be a lot of chaos if pairs are standing close to each other. Make sure this activity is facilitated in a spacious environment where pairs can move away from each other to avoid disturbance.

Virtually: For virtual facilitation break out rooms can be a good option.

Add your personal touch of creativity to the activity to craft your unique version.

Shiny Star And Stinky Fish

This activity brings balance, it enforces the participants to think about the positive and negative aspects of the project, topic, or a sprint.

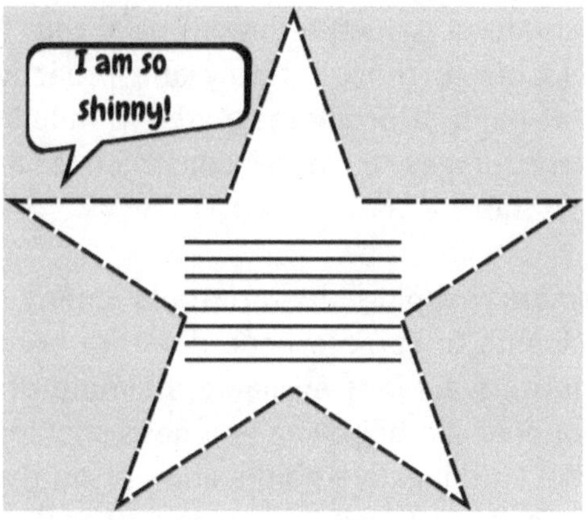

The stinky fish concept and image is inspired from the MIRO template. I have combined it with the Shiny Star to bring a balance.

Stinky Fish: The "Stinky Fish" concept encourages participants to address and discuss the negative or challenging aspects of a topic or situation. It's a way to acknowledge and tackle potential issues or obstacles in a proactive and constructive manner.

Shiny Star: The "Shiny Star" represents the positive aspects, strengths, or opportunities related to the topic. It highlights what's working well and what can be leveraged to achieve success or improvement.

By incorporating the "Stinky Fish" and "Shiny Star" concept into the prep-work for events, meetings, or discussions, you create a structured and balanced framework for participants to think critically and proactively about the topic at hand. It promotes a well-rounded understanding and encourages a more constructive and productive conversation.

In-person: Keeping the printouts handy or asking the participants to come prepared with a printout. Specify if the printers are not available a simple drawing or even sticky notes can help. The emphasis should be sharing the positive and negative points and not on the format. Keep an eye on your emails, some participants might also send back the filled in document back to you. Make sure you can print these out on their behalf.

Virtual: In case you are sending a digital copy, make sure participants can edit it. Use word documents rather than

PDF or PNG files. Add clear instructions on how to edit the digital copy. Avoid sharing a common document, most of the participants would end up using the same document rather than creating their own copies.

Add your personal touch of creativity to the activity to craft your unique version.

Roll a story

"Roll a Story" is a creative and engaging activity that can lead to entertaining and insightful stories.

Roll a Story

Roll a die three times to pick a character, setting, and problem.
Then, use these to create a 60 sec story with a morale

	Character	Setting	Problem
⚀	A zoo keeper	In a dark forest	Finds a magic wand
⚁	A beautiful princess	On a ship	Gets stuck in a fire
⚂	A big bear	In a desert	Meets a big monster
⚃	An old man	In a hidden cave	Gets lost
⚄	A friendly alien	At a farm	Is chased by a wolf
⚅	A brave policeman	On a spaceship	Sees a ghost

As a facilitator you can create your own sheet or use the one that I have shared in the above image.
While facilitating this group activity the participants roll a die three times to randomly select a character, setting, and problem.
Character: The first roll of the die selects the character.
Setting: The second roll determines the setting.
Problem: The third roll reveals the problem.
Every participant gets a total of 90 seconds. 30 seconds of thinking time and 60 seconds to narrate the story with a moral. The key is to keep the story short and simple.

This "Roll a Story" activity not only sparks creativity but also encourages participants to reflect on the deeper meaning of their stories, making it a fun and enriching experience for all involved. By changing the characters, settings and problems to align with a theme you can make this activity more involving for the participants.
It enhances engagement and encourages deeper reflection on how to address challenges and make improvements within their respective contexts. This adaptability makes the activity a valuable tool for a wide range of learning and team-building scenarios.

For example: You can change the characters to different types of roles in a team or organisation, change the settings to actual situations a team encounters and by replacing the problems with team challenges. You can use this activity in multiple setups.
I have provided an example of a Scrum Team through including Team Roles, Scrum Events, and some of the common difficulties that teams experience. You can modify this sheet to address team-specific issues.

Roll a Story

Roll a die three times to pick a character, setting, and problem.
Then, use these to create a 60 sec story with a morale

	Character	Setting	Problem
1	A Developer	During Sprints	Missing JIRA updates
2	A Product Owner	In Refinements	Micromanage
3	A Stakeholder	During planning	Skips meeting unannounced
4	An Engineering Manager	At a team meeting	Priority change
5	A Tech Lead	Review	Communication barrier
6	A Team Member	Retrospective	Scope creep

In-person: If this activity is facilitated in-person, all we need is a printed copy of sheet, a dice and some interesting participants. Make sure you make the participants sit in a circle facing each other. Place a table in the middle to keep the sheet and roll the dice. Make sure the chairs and the table are at a comfortable distance.

Virtually: During virtual facilitations, you can use digital tools for rolling the dice, making sure the sheet of paper is visible throughout the activity. Use of a digital timer can be helpful for time management.

Thinking Page

Add your personal touch of creativity to the activity to craft your unique version.

What Do You Need...

"What Do You Need.. *To Make This Project A Success*". The second part of the question helps set the stage for the conversation.

You can change the second part of the question to change the context. For Example: What Do You Need.. *To Finish The Current Task?* or What Do You Need.. *To Reach Your Goal?* What Do You Need.. *To Meet The Customer Expectations?* or What Do You Need.. *To Overcome The Current Challenge?*

The focus is on trying to understand the participant's needs and what they expect in order to reach a certain target or achieve a goal. This approach encourages participants to reflect on their unique needs and paves the way for meaningful conversations and actionable solutions.

In-person: During In-Person events you get to experience a deeper connection while having these conversations. You have access to non-verbal cues like body language, facial expressions, and gestures. These cues convey emotions, intent, and nuances that can be essential for effective communication.

Virtual: This does not imply that you won't benefit from inquiring about needs in a virtual setup. Virtual communication tools have improved significantly and offer unique benefits such as accessibility, remote collaboration, and convenience.

Thinking Page

Add your personal touch of creativity to the activity to craft your unique version.

Something nice to say...

Each team member gives a compliment about a fellow team member. He or she begins, "I have something nice to say about *<Name>*," and then offers a complement.

It's a wonderful way to foster a positive team culture and celebrate the unique qualities and contributions of each team member. This activity goes beyond formal recognition and allows colleagues to express genuine compliments and appreciation.
Whether it's for birthdays, farewells, or just celebrating someone's outstanding work, it brings a warm and inclusive spirit to the team. It reminds us that taking a moment to appreciate and uplift one another can create a supportive and harmonious work environment.

In-person: During special occasions like birthdays or celebrating achievements. Ask the participants to stand in a circle and let the individual who is been celebrated stand in the middle of this circle. Now let the participants standing in the circle start complementing this individual who is standing in the middle using the phrase "I have something nice to say about *<Name>...*". You can also use tagging technique or just go in clockwise or anticlockwise directions.

Virtual: To make it interesting you can ask the special individual to wear a hat or hold some prop. It adds a dramatic effect. Tagging works well in a virtual setup. One of the participants can start and tag the next person who can complement and the process of tagging and complementing continues till everyone is done.

Add your personal touch of creativity to the activity to craft your unique version.

Retrospective Templates

Retrospective Templates

Retrospective templates are predefined structures or frameworks that help in several ways to capture insights, derive action items, focus on improvements, foster collaborations, and promote engagement.

Retrospectives begin with creating a safe environment. This is not a one-day, one-meeting thing. It is an ongoing process of establishing and continuing to create a safe space for the team. A place where everyone feels comfortable and can speak their mind. It fosters trust and encourages open communication.

Retrospective Templates can be broadly divided into the below types:

Types of Retrospectives

Open Retrospectives

- In an open retrospective, there is no predefined agenda or specific topic to focus on.
- The team has the freedom to discuss any aspect of their work, team dynamics, processes, or challenges.
- The discussions are open-ended, allowing team members to bring up any relevant issues, share their experiences, and propose improvements.
- Open retrospectives provide a space for broader discussions and the opportunity to address a wide range of topics that may not fit into a specific retrospective template.
- This format encourages flexibility and creativity in

exploring different aspects of team performance and collaboration.

Topic specific Retrospectives

- In a topic-specific retrospective, the focus is narrowed down to a specific area or theme.
- The retrospective is designed around a predefined topic or challenge that the team wants to address or improve.
- The discussions and activities revolve around that particular topic, allowing for a deep dive into specific issues, processes, or practices related to the chosen theme.
- Topic-specific retrospectives provide a more focused approach to problem-solving and improvement in a specific area of concern.
- Examples of topic-specific retrospectives include retrospectives focused on communication, psychological safety, improving refinements, or reviews.

Both open retrospectives and topic-specific retrospectives have their benefits and can be used based on the team's needs and objectives. Open retrospectives provide flexibility and the opportunity to explore various areas, while topic-specific retrospectives allow for a deeper analysis of specific challenges. The choice between the two depends on the team's goals, the nature of work, or the improvements the team wants to address.

Team Retrospectives

Retrospectives are a valuable tool for continuous improvement, and they should not be limited to just sprint or work-related topics. Team retrospectives offer a broader perspective on the team's dynamics, collaboration, and overall effectiveness. Team Retrospectives can be both Open or Topics specific. Here are some key points to emphasise when conducting a team retrospective.

- **Holistic Assessment:** Encourage the team to look beyond the specific tasks or projects they've been working on. A team retrospective provides an opportunity to assess the overall health and performance of the team.
- **Team Dynamics:** Explore how the team members interact with each other. Are there clear communication channels? Is there a sense of trust and psychological safety within the team? How are conflicts resolved? These are important aspects to consider.
- **Strengths and Weaknesses**: Identify and celebrate the team's strengths and successes. This positive reinforcement can boost morale and motivation. Simultaneously, acknowledge weaknesses and challenges to work on them collaboratively.
- **Comfort Level:** Discuss the comfort level within the team. Do team members feel safe expressing their ideas and opinions? Are there any barriers to open communication that need to be addressed?
- **Collaboration:** Evaluate how well team members are collaborating and whether they are effectively

leveraging each other's strengths. Explore opportunities for better synergy and coordination.

- **Safe Space:** Ensure that the retrospective is conducted in a safe and non-judgmental environment. Team members should feel comfortable sharing their thoughts and concerns without fear of reprisal.

THINKING PAGE

Add your personal touch of creativity to the activity to craft your unique version.

AFLI (Assumptions | Facts | Learnings | Improvements)

This retrospective template is designed to facilitate a discussion around assumptions made during a project or a specific period, uncover the facts that challenge those assumptions, identify key learnings from the experience, and generate ideas for improvements moving forward. It provides a structured approach to reflecting on past events and leveraging them for future growth and success.

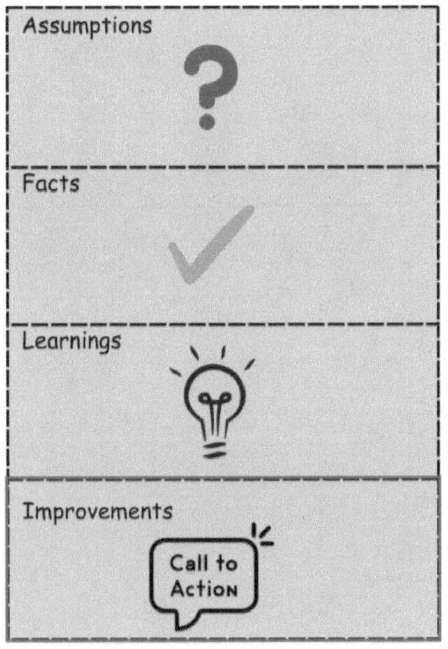

Facilitation

Assumptions

Ask the team members to write down all the assumptions with which they started the project, sprint, feature, or topic. Also, write down all the Assumptions they had or continued to have throughout the period of the project, sprint, feature, or topic on sticky notes. Group similar sticky notes and try to find a theme or pattern. Add these sticky notes under the Assumptions sections.

Facts: The next step is to initiate discussion to uncover the Facts that challenge these Assumptions. Note these facts on stickies and add them under the Facts sections.

Learnings: After noting down the facts, ask the participants to share their Learnings either individually or in groups based on the size of the team. Record these learnings on sticky notes and place them under the Learnings section.

Improvements: Based on the Assumptions, Facts, and Learning encourage the participants to brainstorm in order to derive actionable improvements. Note them on sticky notes and add them under the Improvement sections. Depending on the number of action items, prioritise them to determine the next steps.

Conclude the Retrospective by summarising the key takeaways. Ensure the team has a clear plan and everyone is on the same page.

THINKING PAGE

Add your personal touch of creativity to the activity to craft your unique version.

Book Cover

This retrospective activity is a creative and engaging way to check in with your team on various topics, whether it's related to a sprint, quarterly roadmap, or personal achievements. This activity encourages participants to express their thoughts and ideas using a book cover format, making it visually interactive and stimulating creativity.

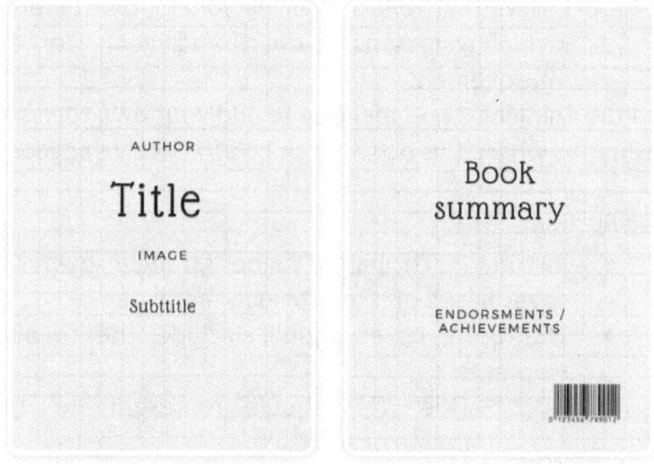

The activity is to visually represent and discuss the topic using a book cover format.

Topics for book cover activity:

- **Quarterly Roadmap**: Participants design book covers representing the key objectives and focus areas for the upcoming quarter.
- **Sprint Review**: Each participant creates a book cover that symbolises the achievements and highlights of the recent sprint.
- **Personal Achievements**: Participants design book covers that reflect their personal accomplishments and goals.

- **Career Development**: Team members create book covers that reflect their career goals, aspirations, and the skills they want to develop.
- **Innovation and Creativity**: Use the activity to spark creative thinking by having participants design book covers that symbolise innovative ideas or concepts.
- **Personal Growth**: Team members design book covers that reflect their personal growth journey, including lessons learned and goals for self-improvement.

On the Thinking Page, feel free to add your own topics and scenarios where this activity can be effectively applied.

Facilitation:

- Instruct participants to design their own book cover based on the provided template.
- The book cover should include the following elements:
    - Title: This should represent the main theme or topic.
    - Author: In this case, the author is the participant.
    - Subtitle: A short phrase or description that adds context.
    - Front Cover Image: An image that symbolises or represents the topic.
    - Book Summary: A brief summary of what the book is about (pertaining to the chosen topic).
    - Endorsements or Achievements: What the "book" (topic) has achieved or aims to achieve.
- Time box creativity: Allow participants some time

to get creative and design their book cover. They can use drawings, words, or a combination of both.

- Presentation and Discussion: After designing their book covers, have participants present and discuss them with the group. Each participant can explain their design choices, including the title, subtitle, image, and book summary. Encourage open discussions and ask follow-up questions to delve deeper into their perspectives.
- Reflect and Share: After each presentation, invite other participants to share their thoughts and reactions to the book cover and the topic it represents.
- Group Discussion: Conclude the activity with a group discussion about the topic. Summarise key insights, ideas, and any common themes that emerged during the presentations.

"Book Cover" activity can also serve as a quick visual check-in activity for teams to express their thoughts and perspectives on a variety of topics. It provides a creative and engaging way to capture team member's sentiments and insights quickly.

THINKING PAGE

Add your personal touch of creativity to the activity to craft your unique version.

Hot Air Balloon

It is one of my favourite Retrospective activities. The Hot Air Balloon is a combination of retrospective and futurespective and is a creative and comprehensive way to assess past activities while also looking forward to the future. It uses the metaphor of a hot air balloon, sandbags, storm clouds, sunshine, patchwork, and holes to represent various aspects of the team's journey.

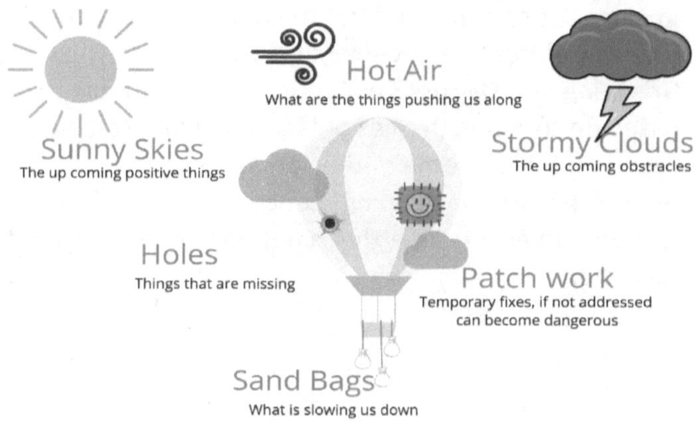

Facilitation:

Introduction: Introduce the purpose of the retrospective and futurespective, which is to assess past work and proactively plan for the future. Explain the metaphor of the hot air balloon, sandbags, storm clouds, sunshine, patchwork, and holes.

Template Explanation: Show the visual template to the team, which includes sections for "Sandbags," "Hot Air", "Storm Clouds", "Sunshine", "Patch Work" and "Holes". Clarify that "Sandbags" represent factors that have been holding the team back, while "Hot Air" represents what has been driving the team forward. “Storm Clouds” symbolise potential negative events or risks on the horizon, “Sunshine” represents positive events or opportunities. “Patch Work” represents the temporary fixes that, if not addressed, can become dangerous, and “Holes” represents the missed opportunities.

Individual Reflection: Ask each team member to reflect on the current sprint or project and write down their thoughts on sticky notes. Ask them to share it with the entire group.

Voting: Voting can help filter the noise and help focus on a few crucial topics the team wants to address.

Grouping and Discussion: Group the sticky notes together based on common themes or factors. Facilitate a discussion based on the outcome of the voting.

Action Items: Developing concrete action items with owners can ensure that this is not only discussed and then forgotten.

Thinking Page

Add your personal touch of creativity to the activity to craft your unique version.

Psychological Safety

Psychological safety is the belief that you won't be punished or humiliated for speaking up with ideas, questions, concerns, or mistakes. At work, it's a shared expectation held by members of a team that teammates will not embarrass, reject, or punish them for sharing ideas, taking risks, or soliciting feedback.

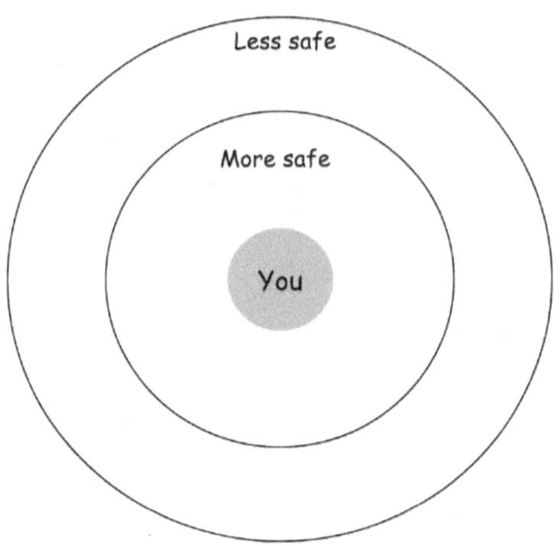

Trust is a by-product of psychological safety. I believe team members who are courageous and open, respect one another's boundaries, and are committed and focused on attaining a common objective based on trust help form a safe environment.

Facilitation

- Request that each team member spend 10 minutes writing down the most significant behaviours they have encountered while working as a team, both positive and negative
- Let them place these sticky notes based on how these behaviours make them feel. Within the range of More safe and Less safe the further the sticky is placed from the inner circle "You", the less safe the behaviour is. The closer the sticky is placed to the inner circle, the more safe the behaviour is.
- Let every individual team member explain the behaviour and how it affects them when discussing the negative behaviours. It is important to explicitly specify the alternative expected behaviour. To give a clear guideline.
- Team members are then encouraged to ask clarifying questions and think of alternatives or improvements. Note them in the form of action items.

Ask the participants to start mapping sticky notes with specific behaviours depending on how they made them feel. Did it make them feel safe, or did it threaten or endanger their safety?

After the participants are done listing these behaviours, start the discussion. The goal of this discussion is not to vent; the focus was to find an alternative expected behaviour instead of the toxic behaviour that was listed in the outermost circle. It also created an opportunity to highlight the behaviours that make individuals feel safe.

This helps make sure the good behaviours get rooted within the team.

The action points or alternative behaviours are then noted on the coloured sticky notes. When they encountered or experienced toxic or unhealthy behaviour, participants are supposed to communicate the expected behaviour. This is important since what might be normal for one person might be affecting the other person in a negative manner. For example, checking your phone during 1-to-1 conversations can be normal for one person, but that could be offensive to the other, who expects you to be present during the conversations.

These improvements could be simple or more intense, depending on the team dynamics and composition.

The quest to establish safety shouldn't stop here. Periodic checks or feedback from the team will help identify the impact of these discussions and action items. Employee experience in such situations could be key to forming close-knit, committed teams with high trust, engagement, and collaboration. It also nurtures an inclusive culture.

THINKING PAGE

Add your personal touch of creativity to the activity to craft your unique version.

SPOT Light: to maintain focus

This activity is recommended for maintaining focus. It can be used for topic-specific retrospectives, clearing backlogs, managing to-do lists, defining initiatives, and creating a plan to meet the objective. It supports retaining the focus on the core purpose and avoiding drifting away from it.

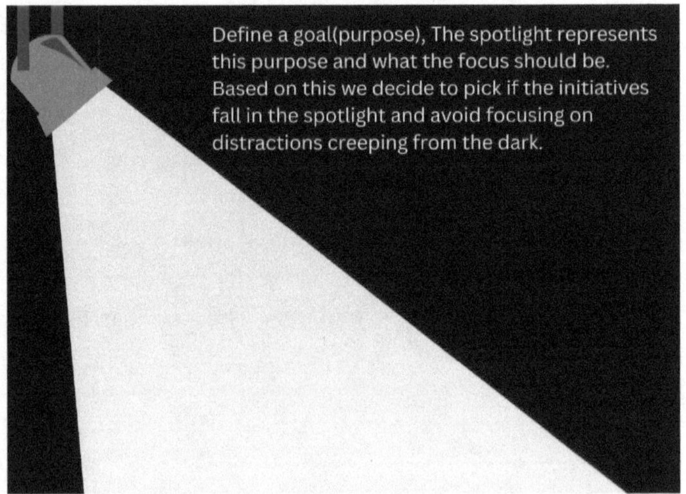

Facilitation

Begin by explaining the activity's purpose and how it will help maintain focus and prioritise tasks. Mention the distinction between what's necessary and what's nice to have.

Discussion: Pick one card or initiative at a time and introduce it to the team. Encourage a short discussion to decide if it adds value and contributes to the purpose.

Placement: Depending on the team's decision, categorise the initiatives:

- **In the Spotlight**: These are the initiatives that directly contribute to the core purpose and must be prioritised.
- **In the Darkness**: These are initiatives that don't directly align with the core purpose and can be set aside.
- **On the Border**: Some initiatives may fall in-between, not high priority but good to have.

Timelines: The time required for this activity depends on the number of initiatives and the depth of the discussions. Clear alignment on the core purpose is crucial for efficient decision-making.

THINKING PAGE

Add your personal touch of creativity to the activity to craft your unique version.

Hiking Retrospective

This template can be an option when the team has experienced a challenging sprint, project, or specific period of time.

Facilitation

The hiking retrospective template concentrates on 4 questions.

The weather — Represents the team's work environment, and how it makes them feel. Consider the hailstones example mentioned above.

The boulders — Represent the things that prevented you from achieving your goal. This can be inter-team dependencies, technical challenges, mid-sprint changing priorities, or communication barriers.

The equipment — These are things that helped you

during hiking to reach your goal. You can talk about people, events, tools, or anything else that supported you on the journey.

The missing stuff — These are things that were not there and having them in place could have made it better or more fun. Hypothetical examples can be a missing map, binoculars, great food, campfire, toilets, etc. A relatable real example could be minimum stories getting rolled over, quick MR's approvals, collaborative colleagues, and great inter-team communication.

Missing factors are areas for improvement.

- Set up the retrospective: Prepare a space for the team to gather and provide sticky notes and markers for each team member.
- Introduce the four areas: Explain the purpose of each category—weather, boulders, equipment, and missing stuff. Encourage the team to reflect on their experiences and generate ideas for each category.
- Individual input: Give the team members time to write their thoughts on sticky notes, placing them in the corresponding category. Each team member should contribute their own ideas and experiences.
- Share and provide context: Once everyone has added their sticky notes, go through each category one by one. Ask each individual to explain or provide context for their sticky notes, giving others a clear understanding of their perspective.

- Foster discussion: Encourage the team to discuss the topics raised during the explanation phase. This can involve asking questions, seeking clarifications, sharing similar experiences, or exploring potential solutions.
- Derive improvement action items: As the discussion progresses, identify key themes, patterns, or common areas for improvement. Collaboratively derive action items or strategies that can help address the issues identified. Ensure that these action items are specific, actionable, and measurable.
- Additional topics and voting: If new topics emerge during the discussion phase and the team feels overwhelmed by the number of ideas, consider using voting to prioritise which topics to focus on further. Each team member can vote on the topics they consider most important or impactful.
- Summarise and document: Summarise the main points, action items, and decisions made during the retrospective session. Ensure that these are documented for future reference and accountability.

By addressing these four categories in a retrospective, teams can engage in meaningful discussions about their work environment, challenges, supportive factors, and areas for improvement. This template provides a structured framework to assess past experiences, learn from them, and make necessary adjustments for future success.

THINKING PAGE

Add your personal touch of creativity to the activity to craft your unique version.

Abstract ladder - Why | What | How

The Abstract Ladder template, as described in the book "Good Talk" by Daniel Stillman, aims to establish a conversation interface that promotes more collaborative and effective discussions.

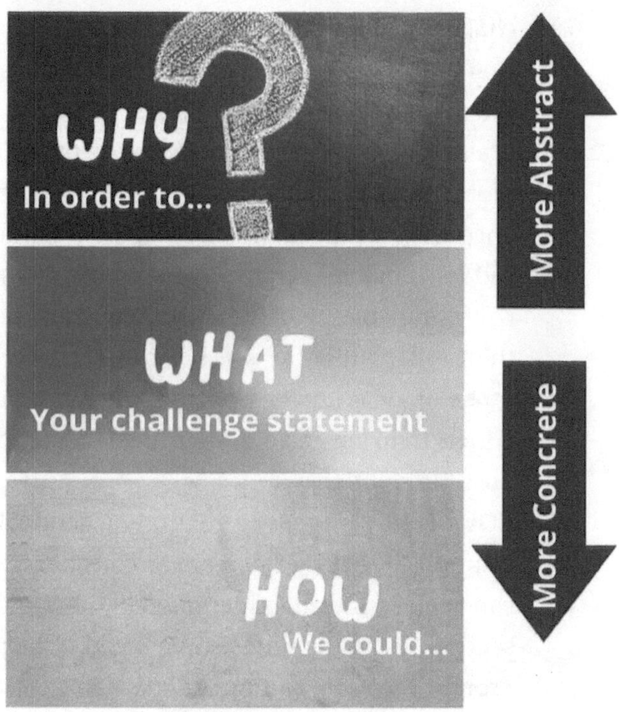

This template can be used for topic-specific retrospectives. Start with explaining the challenge.

Facilitation

- WHAT: Start by clearly identifying and writing down the current challenge or goal that the team wants to address. This serves as the initial focus of the conversation.
- WHY: Allow the team members to think individually and reflect on why they believe this challenge is critical. Provide sticky notes and ask them to write down reasons or motivations using the phrase "In order to..." This encourages brainstorming and helps surface the underlying motivations behind addressing the challenge. By encouraging individual thinking, the Abstract Ladder template helps prevent crowd mentality or conformity bias. Participants are encouraged to think independently, which can lead to a broader range of ideas and perspectives. This promotes critical thinking and a more robust exploration of possible solutions.
- HOW: Shift the focus to generating actionable solutions by asking the team to consider how they can achieve the goals identified in the WHY section. Using the phrase "We could..." helps prompt the team to suggest concrete actions or strategies. This step helps identify actionable steps or approaches to address the challenge as a team.

By combining individual thinking and team brainstorming, you create an environment that promotes both independent thought and collective intelligence.

THINKING PAGE

Add your personal touch of creativity to the activity to craft your unique version.

Divest | Invest | Loan

This retrospective activity focuses on things from which the team expects to divest, things that the team wants to invest and things they know can make an impact but need help with.

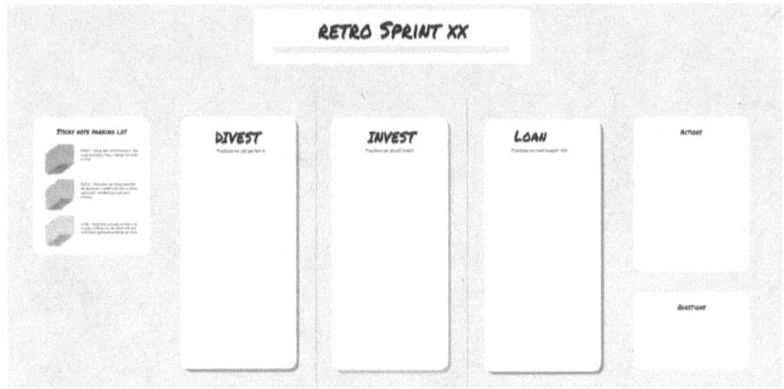

Facilitation

- Begin the retrospective meeting by explaining the purpose and the process to the team.
- Ask team members to individually reflect on the recent sprint or project iteration and write down their thoughts on sticky notes:
- Red (**Divest**): *Practices we need to say bye to.* Identify what should be stopped or divested from because it's not working well or no longer providing value.
- Green (**Invest**): *Practices we need to invest in.* Highlight what should be started or invested in to bring value or improve processes.
- Pink (**Loan**): *Practices we need help with.* Identify areas where help is needed to improve performance.

- Once team members have added their sticky notes, facilitate a group discussion section by section (Divest, Invest, Loan). Encourage team members to share their thoughts, one sticky note at a time. Facilitate a discussion around each sticky note, allowing others to provide input or clarify their points of view.
- Summarise the key takeaways for each section after discussing all the sticky notes in that category. Identify action items that can be derived from the discussion for each category. Note the action items in a dedicated area on the retrospective template.
- To prioritise action items and filter out less critical issues, consider using a voting mechanism (e.g., dot voting or thumbs-up stickers).
- Define action items clearly, specifying who will be responsible for each, and set a timeframe for completion. Prioritise smaller changes or improvements that are within the team's control to boost team morale.

THINKING PAGE

Add your personal touch of creativity to the activity to craft your unique version.

Mindmap

Mind mapping is a powerful technique for organising information and generating creative ideas visually. It was popularised by Tony Buzan.

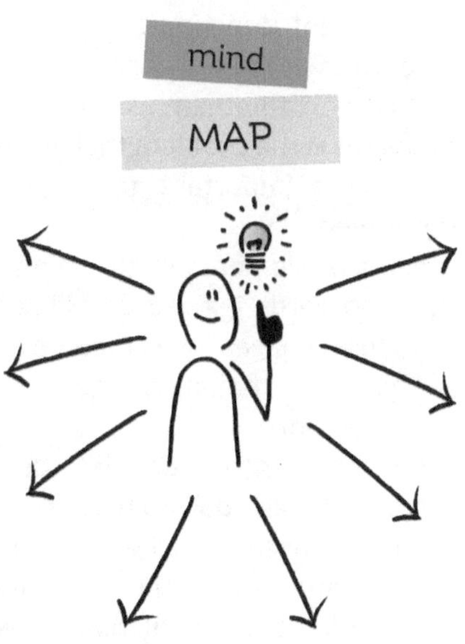

Mind mapping is a versatile technique that can be used for various purposes, such as:

Note-taking, brainstorming, problem-solving, creative endeavours, decision-making, studying. It has also proved to be an effective technique for topic specific retrospectives.

Facilitation

- Start by adding the main topic of discussion at the centre of a white board. This can be the problem at hand, a theme, topic or just a concept the team wants to explore. It acts as the focal point of the mind map.
- Ask the team to brainstorm and add the gathered data to the mind map using branches fanning out in different directions. These branches represent subtopics or related concepts.
- To support the team ask powerful questions such as: what is the problem that we are trying to solve, why is it important to solve it, what can be improved.
- Keep the elements of the mind map concise and use keywords instead of full sentences. You can also use images or symbols to represent ideas, which can enhance memory retention and engagement.
- Add sub-branches and let the mind map grow organically as you brainstorm or explore a topic. Connect these branches and elements based on the connections. This will help explore the association or inter-relation between the elements of the mind map. It provides a visual representation of related elements.

Thinking Page

Add your personal touch of creativity to the activity to craft your unique version.

The Sprint Itinerary

"The Sprint Itinerary" Retrospective is an excellent approach for focusing on future sprint planning and improvements based on lessons gained from the current sprint or previous sprints. The facilitator can also offer data in the form of metrics such as velocity, team capacity, burn down chart, and ticket cycle time during this retrospective.

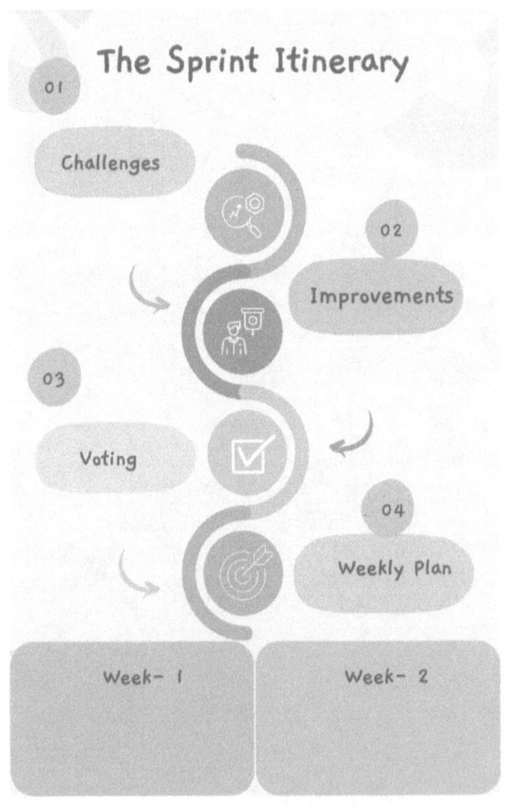

Facilitation

- **Data Review:** The retrospective begins with a review of relevant data and metrics, such as velocity, team capacity, burn-down charts, and ticket cycle times. These metrics provide a factual basis for the discussion.
- **Identification of Challenges and Lessons:** The team identifies challenges, obstacles, and lessons learned from the data and their experiences during the sprint. This part of the retrospective helps in recognizing areas for improvement.
- **Improvement Ideas:** Team members are encouraged to suggest improvement ideas based on the challenges and lessons identified. These ideas can range from process changes to adjustments in team dynamics. It's important that each participant clearly articulates the challenge their improvement idea addresses and how it will help resolve it.
- **Discussion Session:** During this discussion, participants can elaborate on their improvement ideas, providing context and reasoning for why they believe these ideas will be effective in addressing the identified challenges.
- **Voting:** After the discussion, the team collectively votes to determine which of the suggested improvements should be implemented. This voting process allows for consensus-building and prioritisation.
- **Weekly Plan Creation:** The team collaboratively creates a weekly plan that includes the chosen improvement items. This weekly plan serves as a timeline for when each action should be taken. It provides a clear schedule for addressing the

identified challenges and making improvements.

By following these steps, “The Sprint Itinerary” Retrospective not only helps teams reflect on their past performance but also empowers them to actively plan for the future. The combination of data-driven insights and collaborative improvement ideas ensures that the team's retrospectives result in concrete actions and continuous growth. This approach aligns well with Agile principles and fosters a culture of adaptation and improvement.

THINKING PAGE

Add your personal touch of creativity to the activity to craft your unique version.

Sugar & Salt

The concept of using the Sugar and Salt analogy for feedback is both creative and effective. It provides a framework for team members to deliver feedback that is both positive and constructive, emphasising the importance of balance and the unique value of each type of feedback.

This is a non-sprint related retrospective it focuses on the team.

Facilitation

- Using two paper cups, one labelled "Sugar" and the other labelled "Salt" for everyone is a simple and tangible way to represent the concept of positive and constructive feedback. The symbolism of these labels makes it easy for team members to understand the purpose of each cup and encourages them to provide feedback in a balanced manner.
- The "Sugar" cup represents positive feedback, which is the sweetness of recognition and appreciation. When someone does something well or goes above and beyond, their achievements can be acknowledged by placing feedback notes in the Sugar cup. This not only boosts morale but also reinforces the positive behaviours and contributions that the team values.
- The "Salt" cup represents constructive feedback, which is the seasoning that enhances growth and improvement. When there are areas for improvement or behaviours that need adjustment, team members can provide feedback in the Salt cup. This feedback is meant to help individuals identify opportunities for development and make necessary changes.
- Encourage team members to write both "Sugar" (positive) and "Salt" (constructive) feedback for everyone on their team. Encourage them to be specific and clear in their feedback, focusing on behaviours and actions rather than personal traits. After the designated time, instruct team members to place their feedback cut-outs in the appropriate cups (Sugar or Salt) for each team member.
- Begin the feedback sharing session by inviting team

members to share the positive "Sugar" feedback they received. Give team members the option to share the constructive "Salt" feedback they received. Again, stress that this is entirely voluntary, and individuals should only share if they feel comfortable doing so. Team members can also choose to share constructive feedback before sharing the positive feedback and closing on a sweet note.

Add your personal touch of creativity to the activity to craft your unique version.

Let's Craft With Shapes

This retrospective activity is a creative and engaging way to help teams understand and experience the concept of Scrum, specifically focusing on the Sprint cycle. This activity involves planning, execution, review, and reflection to mimic the Agile process while crafting objects from shapes. Material required.

- A unique shape (e.g., star) for each team.
- Glue.
- A stack of white paper.
- Pens (optional) for adding details to objects.

For example: Cut some circles, squares, triangles, rectangles, or any other shapes. Depending on the number and shapes the team has in the bowl, they get to decide what object they can create out of these shapes.

Definition of Done — The requirements listed below must be satisfied for the objects to be marked as completed. Every object at least needs 3 shapes, the shapes can repeat. Do not forget to use the unique shape in one of your objects.

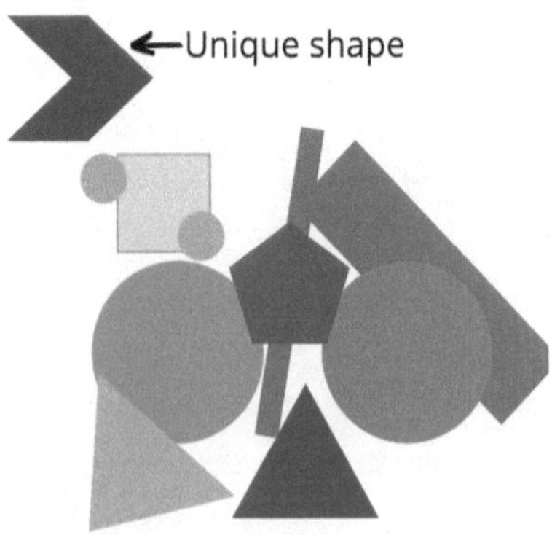

For example, create a sun from a circle and 5 pieces of the triangle. Or create a caterpillar from 6 to 7 circles. Teams can also draw legs and tentacles using a pen so that created objects should be clearly identifiable. Consider if you have one unique piece of a star cut out, the team needs to make use of the star shape combined with more than 2 other shapes to create an object.

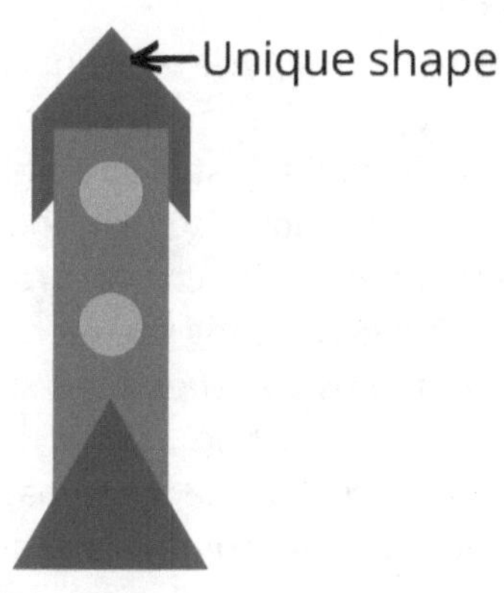

Facilitation

Round 1:

Planning — Each team gets — 3 mins to decide which objects they can create. (Creation means: This includes, assembling and sticking the shapes on the white paper + adding a logo on each white paper creation as part of DoD)

Sprint — At the end of the planning phase, the team needs to confirm how many objects can be created as per DoD. Sprint — The team gets another 3 min to create those objects and complete them as DoD. The team cannot work as a silo; they need to make these objects together.

Review — The facilitator reviews the objects to check if they have been done as per the DoD. The object that is not up to the mark will be discarded. For example — if the team doesn't manage to use the unique shape, all the objects created will be discarded.

Retrospective — Last 3 min are spent reflecting on what could have been done better. What did they estimate to create and what did they achieve in the first sprint? Ask the team to make a note of it.

Round 2:

Repeat the 9 min cycle explained in Round 1.

In the end, ask the team to retrospect and point out the learnings from the first round which helped improve during the second round. Also, ask the team to list what issues they identified during the first round and still repeated the same behaviour during the second round.

Allow all teams to reflect and share their learning during the second portion of the activity. Identify the improvements that the team made as a result of their first-round learning. Encourage the teams to note behaviours they noticed in the first round and didn't manage to improve on in the second.

Round 3: (Optional — If you have time to spare)

Allow teams to watch the third round alternately to see how other teams approached it. This round helps the teams to reflect on what other teams did better or what they could have done better. Let them demonstrate their creations. This activity kicks in the creative mind to help craft some amazing ideas.

Activities like this help in team bonding, making the team do actual sprints in a fun way focusing on all the important factors of Scrum. Tickling the creative nerve to relax the mind, the team learns in a fun way.

THINKING PAGE

Add your personal touch of creativity to the activity to craft your unique version.

Questionnaire

Using a questionnaire template as part of a retrospective is a great way to encourage open and honest communication within a team. It allows team members to voice their questions, concerns, and observations, which can be valuable for continuous improvement.

How long will it take for MR's to be approved?

Should the team be informed about leave schedule?

Who is responsible to update PagerDuty schedule in case of absense?

Is it ok to skip meetings ?

Do we get enough time to focus?

Facilitation:

Design the Questionnaire: Create a questionnaire with a set of questions or prompts related to the team's way of working, communication, collaboration, and other relevant topics. Ensure that the questions are clear and open-ended, encouraging thoughtful responses. Or as a facilitator, open the floor for team members to add their own questions. Encourage them to write down any questions or topics they want to address on sticky notes or a shared digital board.

Group the Questionnaire: Group the question based on relevance. Using voting can be also a good option to focus on the most crucial questions that the team would like to discuss.

Brainstorm: Address the questions and use these questions as a starting point for a meaningful discussion about what went well, what could be improved, and the actions to be taken.

Action Items: Based on the discussion, collaboratively determine action items and assign responsibilities to address the identified issues and implement improvements, revisit the action items and evaluate the progress during upcoming team retrospectives.

Add your personal touch of creativity to the activity to craft your unique version.

The Journey

"The Journey Retrospective" is a valuable and reflective approach to assessing the sprint's progress and overall experience. It allows participants to explore the entire sprint journey, from the start to the end, and it fosters a sense of collaboration in identifying impediments and working on improvements.

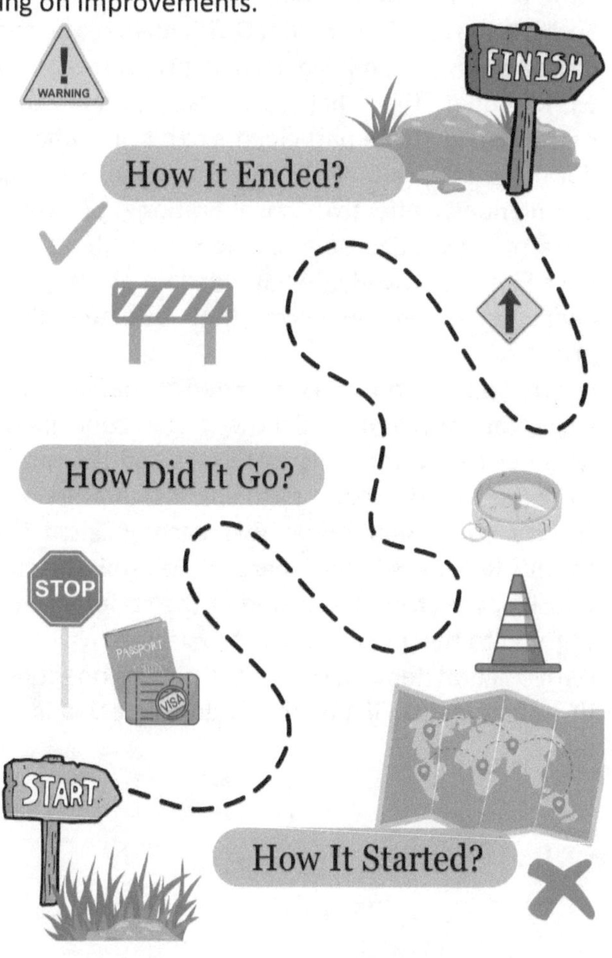

Facilitation:

Sprint Start - "How it Started?": Begin by looking back at how the sprint began. Discuss the initial sprint planning, the goals set, and the overall outlook. Ask participants to share their impressions, expectations, and concerns at the start of the sprint. Consider any challenges or uncertainties that were present at the beginning.

Sprint Progress - "How Did It Go?": Analyse the middle part of the sprint, examining how it progressed. Review the work done, the challenges faced, and the team's performance. Invite participants to discuss what went well during the sprint. This could include successful task completions, effective collaboration, or any positive aspects. Encourage open conversation about what could have been improved or what didn't go as planned. Identify obstacles or impediments that affected the sprint's progress.

Sprint End - "How Was It Ended?": Reflect on the final stages of the sprint and how it was concluded. Discuss whether the sprint goals were met and the quality of the work delivered. Share participant's impressions of the sprint's conclusion. What was accomplished during the sprint's final days? Were there any last-minute challenges? Consider the overall outcome of the sprint and whether it aligns with the initial goals and expectations.

Derive action items based on the discussions conducted by the participants, if possible, add owners and follow up plans.

THINKING PAGE

Add your personal touch of creativity to the activity to craft your unique version.

Roll The Dice And Talk For 1 Min

"Roll the Dice and Talk for 1 Minute" is a creative and engaging retrospective activity that encourages team members to share their thoughts on specific topics.

Talk about refinements conducted during this sprint/project

Talk about stakeholder engagement during this sprint/project

Talk about the dependencies and blockers identified during this sprint/project

Talk about scope changes or scope creeps identified during this sprint/project

The flexibility in how it can be facilitated, either by assigning specific topics to each number or letting each individual roll the dice for a unique topic, adds variety to the activity. Here's how you can facilitate it in both ways:

Facilitations

Option 1: Assigned Topics

Prepare a list of retrospective topics or questions and assign each of them to a number on a standard six-sided die (1 to 6). You can also use 12 questions and use 2 dice.

Gather your team in a meeting or workshop setting.

Choose one team member to start. They roll the die, and based on the number rolled, they have 60 seconds to talk about the topic assigned to that number.

Continue in a clockwise or anti-clockwise order, with each team member taking their turn to roll the die and discuss the topic associated with their roll.

Ensure that everyone has a chance to share their thoughts within the time limit.

Option 2: Unique Topics

Instead of assigning topics to the dice numbers, prepare blank cards or use magnetic cards or a digital tool where team members can write down their own retrospective topics or questions. This allows the team members to decide which topics will be discussed during the Retrospective.

Each team member writes down a unique retrospective topic or question on a card or in the digital tool.

Gather your team in a meeting or workshop setting.

Each team member takes turns rolling the die and then selects a card or topic related to the number they rolled.

They have 60 seconds to talk about the topic or question they have chosen.

Continue this process, ensuring that everyone gets a chance to roll the die and discuss their chosen topic.

The "Roll the Dice and Talk for 1 Minute" retrospective activity offers a structured yet dynamic way for team members to share their thoughts and reflections. It encourages active participation and can lead to diverse discussions, making it an effective tool for retrospectives. The flexibility in choosing between assigned or unique topics allows you to adapt the activity to your team's preferences and needs.

Based on the result of the dice roll and the card that corresponds with it, the person who rolled the dice is expected to respond to the question or discuss the topic at hand. You can inquire as to whether any other participant has anything particular to say, depending on how much time remains.

Additionally, you have flexibility with the 1 minute; based on the team and the timebox, you can prolong the discussion to a few minutes.

Add your personal touch of creativity to the activity to craft your unique version.

PAC-MAN

PAC-MAN is one of the video games that all or most of the team members can relate to. The highlight of this activity is "Remaining Lives" which makes you think not just about the failure or blocker, but helps you take the next step in identifying what you could do differently to turn this failure into success. It helps in having constructive team conversations rather than ranting or venting. The team might also derive interesting action items or ways of working based on the inputs added in the "Remaining Lives" section.

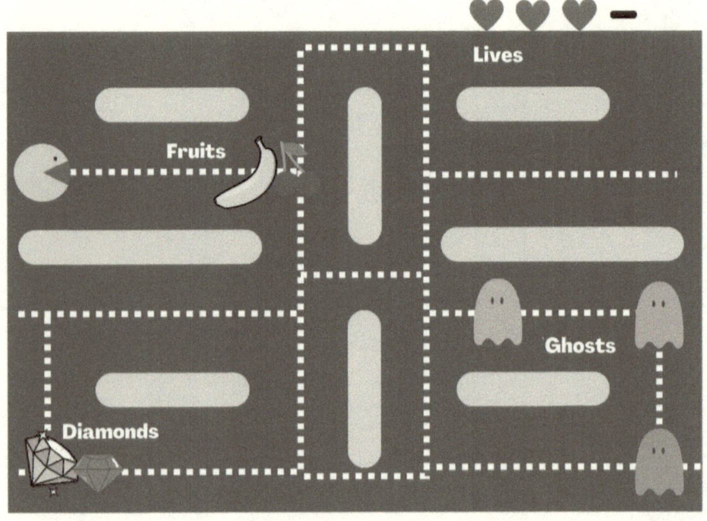

Facilitation

Ghosts: In the Ghosts section of the retrospective board, you identify the things in the last sprint that blocked you from achieving certain goals or have held you back.

Diamonds: These represent bonus rewards. What was a pleasant surprise/bonus during the process and how did it come to be?

Remaining lives: Remaining lives are aspects of the process that you would like to do differently in the next sprint to avoid failure. This section helps you to think one step ahead of what did not work. It makes you think about what you could have done differently to make this work.
Fruits: Fruits are the achievements of this sprint. What made you feel successful? What goals did you achieve?

Introducing the retrospective activity to the team, start with explaining what the 4 areas the team members need to think about to pen down their inputs. If possible, give examples to support the case which helps the team in getting a clear indication of what they are expected to do.

Example: (Remaining lives) A certain story was flagged as blocked due to dependency on another team. What could you have done differently, in order to unblock yourself in such situations?
Try to come up with action items to create detailed plans once everyone has finished sharing.

Add your personal touch of creativity to the activity to craft your unique version.

Snakes and Ladder

Using a Snakes and Ladders gamification approach in a retrospective meeting can be a creative and engaging way to reflect on a sprint or project. It helps participants visualise both their successes and the challenges they faced during the sprint.

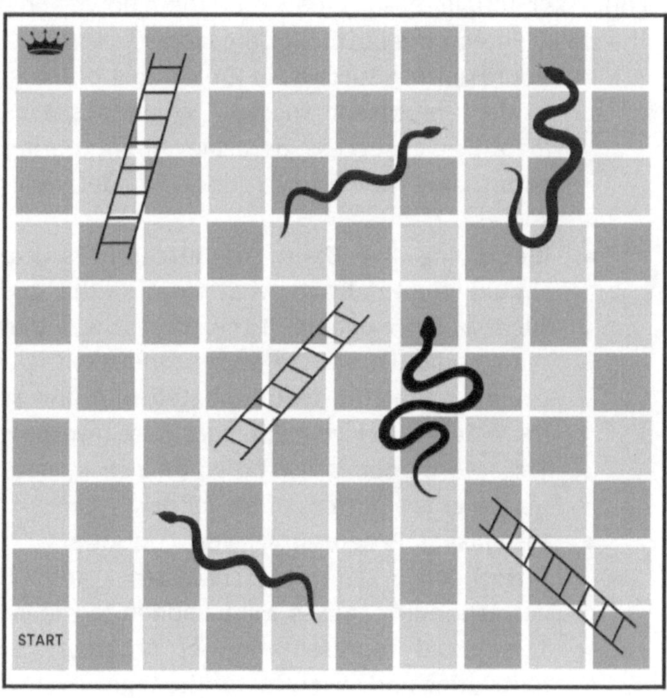

Facilitation

Ladders:

Use 2 or more sticky notes for describing the achievements, first think about the achievement, note it down and place the sticky note at the top of the ladder, now think about what was the cause that pushed you up to achieve it. There could be multiple reasons, now note them down and place the sticky note at the bottom of the ladder.

- **Representing Success:** In the context of the game, ladders represent success. When a participant identifies a success or achievement during the sprint, they should add a sticky note describing the success.
- **Identifying the Cause of Success:** Participants should think about what contributed to this success. For example, if the success was that the team could work more asynchronously, the cause could be that the team updated JIRA and added more details, which helped promote transparency. This information is also noted on a sticky note and placed at the bottom of the ladder.
- **Visualising Progress:** As you continue with the retrospective, more successes and their corresponding causes will be added to the ladder. This visual representation of progress can be motivating and insightful for the team.

Snakes:

Similarly, use 2 or more sticky notes for describing the blockers, first think about the problem, note it down and place the sticky note at the head of the snake, now think about what caused the problem, now note it down and place the sticky note at the tail of the snake.

- **Representing Challenges and Obstacles:** In contrast, snakes represent the difficulties or obstacles faced during the sprint. When a participant identifies a problem or challenge, they should add a sticky note at the head of the snake to describe the problem. This helps to pinpoint and acknowledge the challenges faced.

- **Understanding the Impact:** Participants should also think about the impact of the problem. For instance, if the problem is related to a PagerDuty schedule issue, the impact might be that no one attended incoming requests because there was no one appointed to do so. This impact information is noted on a sticky note and placed at the tail of the snake.
- **Visualising Obstacles:** Just like with the ladders, as the retrospective progresses, more challenges and their corresponding impacts will be added to the snakes. This visual representation allows the team to see the obstacles they have overcome or are still facing and its impact.

Using this approach, the team can see a visual representation of their journey during the sprint or project, which can be both motivating and insightful. It can also help in focusing discussions on what worked well (ladders) and what can be improved (snakes) in a fun and interactive way. It's a great way to foster team collaboration and continuous improvement.

After everyone is done sharing their success and struggles, let the team discuss these topics and derive action items. If there are too many topics to be addressed in the defined timebox go for voting and find the most important topic the team would like to address.

THINKING PAGE

Add your personal touch of creativity to the activity to craft your unique version.

G.R.O.W

The GROW model is a coaching and problem-solving framework that can be applied to various situations, including retrospectives, project management, and personal development. It helps guide discussions and decision-making processes effectively.

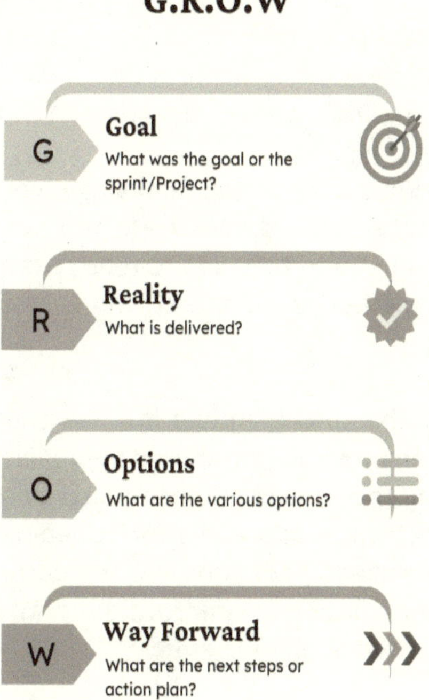

Facilitation

Goal (G): This is the first step where you define and clarify the goal or objective of the sprint or project. What were you aiming to achieve? What was the desired outcome? It sets the direction for the conversation.

Reality (R): In this phase, you assess the current reality or situation. What was actually delivered during the sprint or project? What worked well, and what didn't? What were the key challenges and obstacles encountered?

Options (O): After understanding the current reality, you explore various options or alternatives for moving forward. What can be done to address the gaps or issues identified in the "Reality" phase? This is the brainstorming and problem-solving stage.

Way Forward (W): In the final stage, you establish a plan for the way forward. What are the specific actions and steps that need to be taken to reach the goal or objective? What is the action plan, and who is responsible for each task?

Applying the GROW model in a retrospective or project review can provide a structured approach for analysing and improving the process. It encourages participants to focus on goal setting, reality assessment, generating options, and defining a clear path forward. It's particularly useful for identifying areas for improvement and developing an action plan to address them.

Add your personal touch of creativity to the activity to craft your unique version.

4S

The 4S Retrospective, often referred to as the "Success, Surprise, Sad, Stress" retrospective, is a simple yet effective way to reflect on a project or sprint. It focuses on four key aspects of the team's experience, helping identify achievements, unexpected events, challenges, and areas of stress.

Facilitation

Success (S): Begin with the "Success" category. Ask participants to reflect on and share what went well during the project or sprint. What achievements, accomplishments, or positive outcomes can they identify? Each team member takes turns sharing their successes.

Surprise (S): Next, move on to "Surprise." Encourage participants to think about unexpected events or outcomes, whether positive or negative. What surprised them during the project? This can include both pleasant and challenging surprises.

Sad (S): Transition to the "Sad" category. In this phase, participants discuss what didn't go well or what they found disappointing during the project. This can involve setbacks, failures, or areas where improvements are needed.

Stress (S): Conclude with the "Stress" category. Participants share their experiences of stress or pressure encountered during the project. This can include tight deadlines, resource constraints, or any other sources of stress.

As participants share their thoughts, document their responses on the whiteboard or using a digital tool. You can use separate sections for each category. After all team members have shared their insights, work together to identify common themes or patterns within each category. Discuss the reasons behind these themes and their impact on the project/sprint. Encourage the team to brainstorm action items based on the discussion. What can be done to replicate successes, manage surprises, address areas of sadness, and control stress in future projects? Capture these action items for further planning. Summarise the key takeaways and action items. Ensure that the team leaves the retrospective with a clear plan for improvement in the next project or sprint.

Add your personal touch of creativity to the activity to craft your unique version.

POSTCARD

A "Postcard Retrospective" is a creative and visual way to reflect on a project or sprint. It involves team members creating postcards that capture their thoughts and feelings about the recent work.

Facilitation

You can also use actual POSTCARDS when facilitating this Retrospective in person. Creating a digital copy of a postcard is easy if it's facilitated virtually using digital tools. This is an open format Retrospective where the participants can bring anything to the table for discussion.

- Provide blank postcards (or cardstock) to the participants. Each person's task is to create a postcard that represents their retrospective thoughts and feelings. They can use drawings, words, images, or a combination of these to convey their message.
- Encourage participants to write down key insights or takeaways from the project or sprint on their postcards. These can include lessons learned,

improvements needed, or any other important reflections. This

- After everyone has completed, participants can take turns sharing their postcards with the rest of the team. Each person explains their postcard, discussing what it represents, and any insights written on it. Combine this activity with voting to filter out topics and focus on one or two topics that have emerged during the discussion. Create action items.

The Postcard Retrospective offers a unique and engaging way for team members to express their thoughts and emotions about the project. It encourages creativity and can lead to valuable insights and action items for continuous improvement.

THINKING PAGE

Add your personal touch of creativity to the activity to craft your unique version.

Start - Improve - Continue

This Retrospective template is a valuable framework for teams to reflect on their work and make improvements.

Facilitation

Start: Initiating new processes that may have a positive impact, reduce waste, and contribute to team's success. It consists of both technical and behavioural aspects.

Improve: This includes topics which need improvements that are inefficient, waste time or resources, and can improve the way people feel or the way things work.

Continue: Activities the team has tried and were successful but are not yet part of common practice or team norms.

At the end of the retrospective, ensure that the team identifies specific action items for each phase. These should be concrete, actionable steps that the team will take to implement the changes and improvements discussed. Assign responsibilities and establish timelines for these action items. In subsequent retrospectives, revisit these action items and evaluate their impact on the team's work and progress.

The "Start - Improve - Continue" retrospective is a practical and structured approach that encourages teams to be proactive in identifying opportunities for change, addressing inefficiencies, and ensuring that successful practices become ingrained in the team's routine. It promotes continuous improvement and enhances the team's overall effectiveness.

Add your personal touch of creativity to the activity to craft your unique version.

ABOUT THE AUTHOR

Greetings, I am Yamini. I have a wonderful family of four, including my spouse, my two children, and myself. I have a deep passion for writing, and this book is the culmination of my extensive writing and learning experiences in facilitation. These experiences have been gathered throughout my journey as a Scrum Master and as an individual.

I love to explore new ways to interact with others to make the dialog more impactful and encourage collaboration. Facilitation fascinates me and I love to experiment.

www.ingramcontent.com/pod-product-compliance
Lightning Source LLC
LaVergne TN
LVHW041215150826
845673LV00001B/418

* 9 7 9 8 8 9 2 3 3 3 0 2 3 *